DK EYEWITNESS TRAVEL

TOP 10
BANGKOK

RON EMMONS

![DK] Penguin Random House

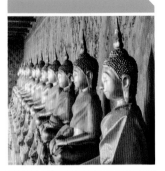

Top 10 Bangkok Highlights

The Top 10 of Everything

CONTENTS

Bangkok Area by Area

Streetsmart

Within each Top 10 list in this book, no hierarchy of quality or popularity is implied. All 10 are, in the editor's opinion, of roughly equal merit.
Throughout this book, floors are referred to in accordance with American usage; i.e., the "first floor" is at ground level.

Front cover and spine *The temple of the Emerald Buddha, or Wat Phra Kaeo, at the Grand Palace*
Back cover *Fruit for sale at Amphawa Floating Market, Bangkok*
Title page *Close-up of a golden Buddha statue in Bangkok*

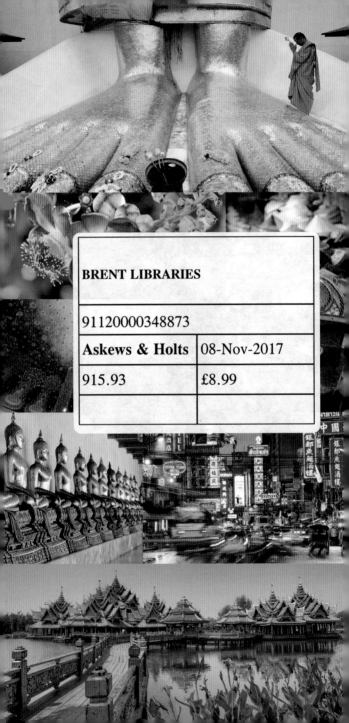

Welcome to
Bangkok

A study in contrasts, Bangkok is simultaneously traditional and modern, noisy and serene. Outside even the glitziest Western-style building, you'll find a small but well-tended shrine respecting the spirit of the land. A city of surprises, it's held together by the famed hospitality of the Thai people. With Eyewitness Top 10 Bangkok, it's yours to explore.

The massive **Chao Phraya River** bisects Bangkok as it flows into the nearby Gulf of Thailand. Along its eastern bank lies the **Old City**, centered around **Rattanakosin**, Bangkok's royal heart, with its spectacular **Grand Palace**, the gleaming treasures of the **National Museum**, and a number of Buddhist temples.

Just downstream lie **Chinatown**'s markets, gold shops, and Taoist shrines. Bangkokians have embraced their riverside roots, and many art galleries and hip pubs take advantage of the low-rise buildings on the river and cool breezes. Inland, you'll find ultramodern downtown hotels, restaurants, and shops, especially among the glass skyscrapers in Silom. Across the river, in **Thonburi**, the unique Khmer-style temple of **Wat Arun** and quiet canals offer a glimpse of a life that could not be more different from the one just over the water.

Whether you're coming for a weekend or a week, our Top 10 guide brings together the best of every aspect of this vibrant Asian capital, from the temples and museums of the Old City to the nightlife Downtown. There's no denying that this city of 9 million can seem bewildering at first. This guide gives you great tips throughout, from seeking what's free to finding that perfect bowl of noodles, plus seven easy-to-follow itineraries, designed to help you visit a clutch of sights in a short space of time. Add inspiring photography and detailed maps, and you've got the essential pocket-sized travel companion. **Enjoy the book, and enjoy Bangkok**.

Clockwise from top: Giant feet of a Buddha image, Wat Indrawiharn; a boat filled with hats in Damnoen Saduak Floating Market; traffic on Yaowarat Road in Chinatown; lakeside pavilion at Muang Boran; Buddha statues, Wat Pho; the Emerald Green Pagoda at Wat Pak Nam, near Khlong Bangkok Yai; a cannonball flower

Exploring Bangkok

Although Bangkok is huge, many of its sights are within walking distance of each other along the river or in nearby Downtown. Using a combination of river boats and mass transit, it's largely possible to avoid the notorious traffic jams. Here are our suggestions for the best things to experience in either two or four days.

Rattanakosin art from the 18th to 20th centuries can be admired in the National Museum.

Wat Phra Kaeo is a complex of prayer halls, towers, and *chedis* (stupas) within the grounds of the Grand Palace.

Two Days in Bangkok

Day ❶

MORNING

Start the day with a visit to the magnificent **Wat Phra Kaeo** and the adjacent **Grand Palace** *(see pp12–15)*, taking time for the excellent **Queen Sirikit Museum of Textiles**. Walk down to the Chao Phraya River and have lunch at one of the small restaurants at **Tha Maharat** *(see p73)*.

AFTERNOON

After lunch, stroll the grounds of **Wat Pho** *(see pp18–19)* and enjoy a back rub in the temple's massage school. Next, visit the **National Museum** *(see pp16–17)*. Have dinner at the **Blue Elephant** restaurant *(see p58)*, then board the boat from Tha Saphan Taksin to Asiatique the Riverfront and take in the **Calypso Cabaret** *(see p51)*.

Day ❷

MORNING

Take a water taxi to **Wat Arun** *(see pp32–3)*, on the Thonburi side of the river, then hop on the Saen Saeb canal boat to **Jim Thompson House** *(see pp30–31)*, the home of the American who revived the Thai silk industry.

AFTERNOON

Browse the shopping malls on **Rama I Road** *(see p89)*, then take in the Thai dance show at **Siam Niramit** *(see p50)*.

Four Days in Bangkok

Day ❶

MORNING

Cross the river to Thonburi to visit the stunning "Temple of Dawn",

Damnoen Saduak Floating Market is renowned for its noodle sellers, who prepare delicious traditional dishes inside *sampan* (rowing boats) on the canal.

bicycle or hire a tuk-tuk to visit the many temples and museums.

AFTERNOON

If time permits, wander around **Wat Pho** *(see pp18–19)* and have a massage, then take in the sunset from **Tha Maharat** *(see p73)*.

Day ❸

MORNING

Wake early to visit the **Damnoen Saduak Floating Market** *(see pp26–7)*.

AFTERNOON

Enjoy the contemporary artworks on display at the **H Gallery** on Silom Road *(see p42)*.

Day ❹

MORNING

Visit **Dusit Park** *(see pp22–3)*, taking in **Vimanmek Palace** and either the **Zoo** or the **Ananta Samakhom Throne Hall**, with its museum.

AFTERNOON

Visit **Jim Thompson House** *(see pp30–31)*, followed by a shopping trip to nearby **Siam Paragon** and the other malls on Rama I Road *(see p89)*.

Wat Arun *(see pp32–3)*, and the **Royal Barge Museum** *(see p96)*.

AFTERNOON

Take in the **National Museum**, **Wat Phra Kaeo**, and the **Grand Palace** *(see pp12–17)*, dine on the river *(see p90)*, then listen to some jazz at **Brown Sugar: The Jazz Boutique** *(see p57)*.

Day ❷

MORNING

Visit the ancient Siamese capital of **Ayutthaya** *(see pp34–7)*. Rent a

Vimanmek Palace, said to be the largest teak building in the world, is home to an extensive collection of royal artifacts.

Top 10 Bangkok Highlights

Buddha statues under a colonnade at the temple of Wat Arun

🔟 Bangkok Highlights

Beguiling and bewildering, spiritual and sensual, Bangkok is one of Asia's most intriguing cities. Its glittering temples and museums overflow with art, while the city's canals and markets reveal the locals' friendly nature. Shopping, dining out, and reveling in the vibrant nightlife should feature high on everyone's itinerary.

Grand Palace and Wat Phra Kaeo ①

This dazzling complex is the pinnacle of perfection in Thai religious art and architecture. An unmissable sight *(see pp12–15)*.

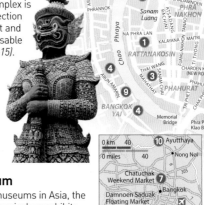

② National Museum

One of the largest museums in Asia, the National Museum displays priceless exhibits, including intricate works of art that clearly document the long and eventful history of Thailand *(see pp16–17)*.

③ Wat Pho

Bangkok's oldest and biggest temple, and formerly a center for public education, Wat Pho houses a massive Reclining Buddha and a school of Thai massage *(see pp18–19)*.

④ Bangkok's Canals

Boats were once the city's main mode of transport. Tour the canals west of the Chao Phraya River to glimpse a vanishing lifestyle *(see pp20–21)*.

Dusit Park ⑤

Learn about the Thai monarchy at this tranquil park studded with royal residences and government offices. It is the ideal spot for a peaceful stroll *(see pp22–3)*.

6 Damnoen Saduak Floating Market

Though designed for tourists, the colorful sights, aromatic smells, and cheerful banter of vendors make a visit to this floating market a delightful experience *(see pp26–7)*.

7 Chatuchak Weekend Market

Bangkok's biggest market offers the chance to pick up a unique souvenir and feel the pulse of Thai culture in the maze of stalls *(see pp28–9)*.

8 Jim Thompson House

This complex is a fine example of Thai teak architecture. The main house remains as it was in the days of Jim Thompson, the man who made Thai silk world-famous *(see pp30–31)*.

9 Wat Arun

With its five distinctive *prangs* (towers), which are often used as a logo of the city, this temple played an important historical role in the development of Bangkok and remains one of its most attractive sights *(see pp32–3)*.

10 Ayutthaya

The ancient city of Ayutthaya is easily visited in a day. Its huge, crumbling *chedis* (stupas) and blissful Buddha images give an idea of the splendor of this former capital *(see pp34–5)*.

TOP 10 ⭐ Grand Palace and Wat Phra Kaeo

In 1782, Rama I (r.1782–1809) established Bangkok as Siam's capital and built Wat Phra Kaeo to house the country's most precious Buddha image. In 1784, he had the Grand Palace built, which became the home of the royal family. No king has resided here since the early 20th century, but the complex is a stunning display of Thai art and architecture and a truly memorable sight.

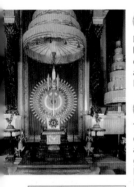

1 Dusit Throne Hall

For many, this building (**left**) is the site's crowning glory, featuring a four-tiered roof and Rama I's teak throne.

2 Amarin Winichai Hall

This building was originally used as an audience hall for foreign guests. Inside, the hall has colorful murals and Rama I's boat-shaped Busabok Mala Throne surmounted by a nine-tiered white canopy. Today the hall is used for state ceremonies and is open to the public on weekdays.

3 Inner Palace

Until the time of Rama VII (r.1925–35), the Inner Palace was inhabited solely by women. All males except the king were forbidden entry. Still closed to the public, it is now a school for girls from prominent families.

4 Chakri Maha Prasat

Occupying center stage in the Grand Palace is the Chakri throne hall (**below**). Built in 1882 by Rama V (r.1868–1910), it fuses Western and Thai architecture. The ashes of Chakri kings are housed here.

NEED TO KNOW

MAP B4 ■ Na Phra Lan Road ■ 02 623 5500 ■ Chao Phraya express boat to Tha Chang

Open 8:30am–4:30pm daily (last entry 3:30pm)

Adm: B500

Queen Sirikit Museum of Textiles: 9am–4:30pm daily (last entry 3:30pm). Adm B150 (museum only)

■ Dress modestly; no sandals, shorts, short skirts, or sleeveless shirts.

■ Keep your ticket for free entry (use within one week) to Vimanmek Palace (*see p23*).

■ Carry water, as the only café is at the end of the tour, next to the Dusit Throne Hall.

⑤ Wat Phra Kaeo

Serving as the royal chapel of the Grand Palace, this complex **(below)** impresses with its slender *chedis* (stupas), glittering mosaics, and the fearsome *yaksha* (giants) by the gates. The *wat* (temple) is Thailand's holiest shrine, though there are no resident monks here *(see pp 14–15)*.

⑦ Aphonphimok Pavilion

This small but attractive wooden pavilion **(right)** was built by Rama IV (r.1851–68) as a royal changing room prior to giving audiences in the adjacent Dusit Throne Hall. Its multi-tiered roof and gold decoration are hallmarks of traditional Thai architecture.

⑨ Wat Phra Kaeo Museum

This museum displays a treasure trove of artifacts salvaged from restoration of the palace, including former costumes of the Emerald Buddha *(see p14)*.

⑩ Queen Sirikit Museum of Textiles

The former Royal Treasury building, constructed from white Italian marble, now houses this museum. On display is ceremonial and modern royal attire, with an emphasis on Thai silk garments, plus pieces from elsewhere in Asia.

⑥ Phaisan Thaksin Hall

This hall is not open to the public and is used only for coronations. It contains the Coronation Chair and the tutelary deity, Phra Siam Thewathirat.

⑧ Siwalai Gardens

These well-kept, picturesque gardens were once used for official receptions. Within the gardens are the Phra Buddha Ratana Sathan, built as a personal chapel by Rama IV *(see p40)*, and Boromphiman Mansion, built by Rama V *(see p40)* for the Crown Prince. It now serves as a guesthouse for visiting dignitaries.

Map of the Grand Palace and Wat Phra Kaeo

ENTERING AND GETTING AROUND THE COMPLEX

All visitors enter by the gate on Na Phra Lan Road, where anyone inappropriately dressed is required to borrow clothes. At the ticket office it is possible to rent an audio-tape or hire a guide to explain the significance of the sights. Visitors usually walk clockwise around Wat Phra Kaeo before exploring the rest of the Grand Palace. Allow about two hours to walk around the site.

Wat Phra Kaeo

Hanuman swallows Phra Ram's pavilion in the Ramakien Murals

1 Ramakien Murals
Stretching over half a mile (1 km) along the cloister walls of the temple, the *Ramakien* murals portray scenes from the Hindu epic *Ramayana* in 178 panels of intricate detail and vibrant color.

2 The Emerald Buddha
Made of jadeite rather than emerald, the most sacred image in the kingdom is just 26 in (66 cm) tall. Thought to have been crafted in Sri Lanka, it was housed in Chiang Rai, Lampang, and Laos before Rama I brought it to Bangkok.

3 Phra Si Rattana Chedi
This glittering, cone-shaped *chedi* (stupa), standing majestically on the upper terrace beside the Phra Mondop, is built of gold tiles in the Sri Lankan style.

Phra Si Rattana Chedi, with its gold tiles

4 Royal Pantheon
The pantheon, one of a trio of tall buildings on the upper terrace, enshrines life-sized statues of the past rulers of the Chakri dynasty *(see p40)*.

5 Model of Angkor Wat
Tucked away behind the Phra Mondop, this model of Angkor Wat was installed by Rama IV *(see p40)*, when Cambodia was under Thai rule.

6 Wihan Yot
Often called "the porcelain *wihan*", this delicately adorned prayer hall stands to the north of Phra Mondop and contains a number of Buddha images.

7 Phra Mondop
This repository for sacred Buddhist texts is on the upper terrace. Its deep-green mosaics are the perfect backdrop for the seated stone Buddhas at each corner.

8 The Bot
The most visited building in the grounds is the *bot* (ordination hall), which contains the much-venerated Emerald Buddha. The interior walls are adorned with murals, and the scent of incense is overwhelming as Thais pay respect to the image that is the country's talisman.

⑨ Hor Phra Nak and Hor Phra Monthien Tham

Flanking the Wihan Yot are the Hor Phra Nak, a royal mausoleum with urns that hold the ashes of members of the royal family, and the Hor Phra Monthien Tham, a library that has particularly fine doors inlaid with mother-of-pearl.

⑩ Chapel of Gandahara Buddha

In the southeast corner of the temple compound stands a small chapel with beautifully painted doors. Usually locked, it contains an image, used in the Royal Ploughing Ceremony (see p64), of the Buddha calling down the rains.

MYTHICAL CREATURES IN THAI TEMPLES

Before visitors get to see the beautifully crafted Buddha images that adorn the *wihan* and *bot* of any Thai temple compound, including Wat Phra Kaeo, they have to pass a panoply of fearsome creatures that act as temple guardians. Most of these beings are from the legendary Himaphan Forest, a kind of Buddhist Shangri-La somewhere in the Himalayan Mountains. These include *singha*, lion-like figures that sit atop gateposts, and *yaksha*, grimacing giants that tower above entrances to the compound. The steps leading up to the *wihan* and *bot* are usually flanked by multiheaded *naga*, serpents that according to legend sheltered the Buddha from a storm while he was meditating. The *hongsa*, a swan-like entity, is often seen perched on the apex of a temple roof. The *kinnari* – half-woman, half-bird – is seen in wall niches or skipping down temple eaves.

Statues of Yakshas, demon giants, stand guard at many Thai temples.

TOP 10
THAI MYTHICAL CREATURES

1 Naga (serpent-like protector of the Buddha)

2 Singha (lion-like temple guardian)

3 Yaksha (giant)

4 Garuda (half-man, half-bird)

5 Erawan (three-headed elephant)

6 Kinnari (half-woman, half-bird)

7 Aponsi (half-woman, half-lion)

8 Hongsa (swan-like figure)

9 Makara (part crocodile, part elephant, part serpent)

10 Mom (dragon-like temple guardian)

TOP 10 ★ National Museum

Thailand's premier museum offers a great introduction to Thai history. Inside, the Buddhaisawan Chapel is one of the country's most precious treasures, as is the Phra Sihing Buddha image it houses. Other highlights include well-preserved fragments of Dvaravati and Srivijaya statues, and the royal funeral chariots.

4 Lanna Art
Several small Buddha images from northern Thailand in the Lanna period (13th to 16th centuries), are on display here.

5 Phra Sihing Buddha Image
One of three such images claiming to be the original, this small but superbly crafted Sukhothai-style sculpture sits on a pedestal in the Buddhaisawan Chapel and is bathed in a golden glow.

1 Buddhaisawan Chapel
This beautiful temple, built in 1787 for the Second King, now sits at the heart of the National Museum complex. Its rich murals, polished floors, gilt Buddha images, and hushed atmosphere make it a star sight **(above)**.

3 Rattanakosin Art
A gallery in the north wing displays art and furnishings from the 18th- to 20th-century Rattanakosin era **(right)**. These pieces combine traditional and Western elements.

2 Ayutthayan Art
Huge, serene Buddha heads, as well as scripture cabinets adorned with scenes of Ayutthaya in its heyday (see pp34–5), are displayed in the Ayutthayan gallery.

6 Red House
A fine example of an Ayutthaya-style teak house, the Red House was originally the home of Rama I's older sister, Sri Suriyen. It has a multitiered roof decorated with beautiful carvings, and the interior contains some antique royal furnishings.

7 2,000 Years of Siamese Art
This gallery, located in the former Sivamokhaphiman Throne Hall, contains superbly displayed and lighted examples of Thai Buddhist art from all the regions of the country.

NEED TO KNOW

MAP B3 ■ Na Phra That Road ■ 02 224 1333 ■ Chao Phraya express boat to Tha Chang ■ www.nmvbangkok.org

Open 9am–4pm Wed–Sun

Adm: B200

■ Join the free guided tours in English, French, German, and Japanese at 9:30am on Wednesdays and Thursdays.

■ The museum covers a big area, but there are seats in shaded corners between galleries where you can take a break.

■ There is a kiosk just inside the entrance selling cold drinks, ice creams, and snacks.

⑧ Sukhothai Art

Sukhothai art (dating from the mid-1200s to the mid-1400s) is often described as the apex of Thai artistic achievement. The flowing lines of walking and sitting Buddha images in the museum fully support this idea **(right)**.

⑨ Royal Funeral Chariots Gallery

The elaborately decorated carriages in this gallery give an idea of the pomp and ceremony that accompany royal funerals. Each of the gilded teak carriages weighs several tons and needs hundreds of men to pull it.

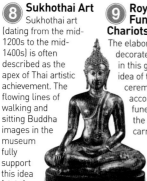

ORIGIN OF THE NATIONAL MUSEUM

The National Museum was originally the Wang Na (Palace of the Front), built in 1782 by Rama I for his younger brother and deputy. However, in 1887, Rama V decided to turn the building into Thailand's first museum so that his subjects could appreciate their rich cultural heritage.

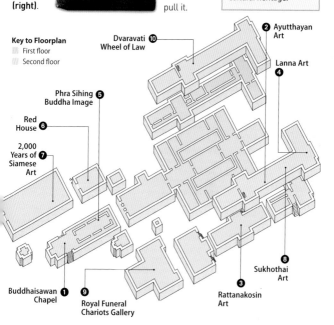

Key to Floorplan

▨ First floor
▨ Second floor

Dvaravati Wheel of Law ⑩

Phra Sihing Buddha Image ⑤

Red House ⑥

2,000 Years of Siamese Art ⑦

Buddhaisawan Chapel ①

Royal Funeral Chariots Gallery ⑨

② Ayutthayan Art

Lanna Art ④

⑧ Sukhothai Art

③ Rattanakosin Art

⑩ Dvaravati Wheel of Law

Dvaravati art flourished from the 6th to the 9th centuries, and this 8th-century stone wheel set above a deer is a great example **(left)**. Located on the second floor of the south wing, it represents the Buddha's first sermon in Sarnath, India.

TOP 10 ⭐ Wat Pho

Bangkok's oldest and largest temple, Wat Pho contains the awe-inspiring Reclining Buddha. Built in the 16th century and reconstructed by Rama I, it is a typical Thai temple, with resident monks, a school, massage pavilions, and a strong community spirit. Around the grounds are a large number of statues and *chedis* (stupas) glittering with mosaics.

3 Feet of the Reclining Buddha

The soles of the feet of the Reclining Buddha are inlaid with 108 *lakshanas*, or auspicious characteristics that identify the true Buddha. Crafted in shimmering mother-of-pearl, these images are a dazzling work of art.

1 Reclining Buddha

The huge Reclining Buddha **(above)**, made of brick, plaster, and gold leaf, fills the *wihan* (assembly hall) in the northwest corner of the compound. Admire its serene expression and its feet, studded with mother-of-pearl inlay.

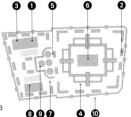

Map of Wat Pho

NEED TO KNOW

MAP B5 ■ Soi Chetuphon ■ 02 226 0335 ■ Chao Phraya express boat to Tha Tien ■ www.watpho.com

Open 8am–6:30pm daily

Adm: B200

■ Most visitors enter from Thanon Thai Wang, next to the Reclining Buddha. However, the southern entrance on Soi Chetuphon allows you to appreciate the rest of the compound in comparative peace before finally arriving at the temple's most popular highlight.

■ Several basic food shops line the western border of the temple.

2 Traditional Massage

Wat Pho is known as a center for traditional medicine and since the 1960s has run what is considered the best massage school in Thailand. Highly trained masseurs are on hand to relieve visitors of their aches and pains. The school also offers 5-day massage courses.

4 Miniature Mountains

On several man-made mounds around the complex are statues of hermits in unusual postures. These are intended to teach people about the healing positions for the body.

5 Medicine Pavilion

In the heart of the complex, the Medicine Pavilion has stone tablets **(left)** indicating the pressure points on the body used during traditional Thai massage.

RECLINING BUDDHAS

A Reclining Buddha appears to be relaxing or even sleeping, but this interpretation could not be farther from the truth. While other images of Buddha standing, sitting, or walking show aspects of his quest to attain Enlightenment, a Reclining Buddha symbolizes his arrival at Nirvana, a state of true all-knowing awareness that is the complete antithesis of relaxation or sleep.

9 Great Chedis

There are about 100 *chedis* in the grounds of Wat Pho **(left)**, but the four most important, in the western courtyard, are the Great Chedis, which enshrine royal ashes and remains of sacred Buddha images. The *chedis* are decorated with porcelain mosaic.

6 The Bot

This ordination hall is Wat Pho's largest building. Inside, the base of the large bronze image of Buddha contains the ashes of Rama I.

7 Farang Guards

Adding a whimsical touch to this temple of learning are huge stone caricatures of Westerners, *farang* in Thai, wearing top hats **(left)**. These guards stand beside the gateways to the inner courtyard of the temple.

8 Schoolkids and Classrooms

In Wat Pho, as in many Thai temples, there is a school for children. At playtime, the compound echoes with their excited screams. Some may even try a few words of English on visitors.

10 Monks and Their Guti

Away from the most popular attractions in the complex, visitors might see monks who work at the temple **(below)**. They live in *gutis* (simple rooms) in a compound to the south of the temple.

TOP 10 ★ Bangkok's Canals

In the 19th century, Bangkok was known as the "Venice of the East," since all transportation was by canal. Today, most of the canals to the east of the Chao Phraya River have been filled in to create new roads. However, the area to the west remains much as it was in the 1800s, with a network of waterways spreading out into the countryside. Here, visitors can get a taste of canalside life and visit attractions such as Wat Arun and the Royal Barge Museum.

1 Floating Vendors

Floating vendors still go from house to house in Thonburi, selling anything from hot food to plastic buckets. There is a better chance of seeing them in the morning.

NEED TO KNOW

Khlong Mon: MAP A5

Khlong Bangkok Noi: MAP A2

Khlong Bangkok Yai: MAP B6

Chao Phraya River: MAP B5

■ To tour the canals, either hire a longtail boat (about B800–1,000 per hour) from any pier, join an organized tour on a larger boat, or take the Saen Saeb Express.

■ Organized tours usually provide refreshments or make a stop where you can buy drinks and food from floating vendors.

3 Khlong Mon

Branching off from the river just north of Wat Arun, this canal leads to an orchid farm where visitors step ashore for a look around before continuing to explore the canal.

4 Boats

It is great fun to sit at a riverside café and watch the pageant of vessels flow by. Huge barges chug downstream, while small ferries nip from bank to bank, and longtail boats with bright awnings **(above)** roar past.

2 Traditional Thai Houses

Traditional houses **(below)** line the canals to the west of the Chao Phraya River. Set on stilts, they usually have an open veranda and pitched roofs.

5 Wat Arun

Established by Rama I, Wat Arun is known as the Temple of the Dawn. Its highlights are the five *prangs* (towers), encrusted with colorful pieces of porcelain *(see pp32–3)*.

Map of Bangkok's canals

6 Royal Barge Museum

This museum *(see p96)* contains a fabulous display of ornamented royal barges **(right)**, which are about 165 ft (50 m) long. Also on display are dioramas of robes worn by royal rowers and information on the use of the barges that appear in royal processions on the river.

7 Khlong Bangkok Noi

Though it is now termed a *khlong*, or canal, this waterway was once the main channel of the Chao Phraya River. Near its entrance is the Royal Barge Museum and a little farther on is Wat Suwannaram, which has some rich murals.

8 Saen Saeb Canal

This canal **(right)** is quite useful for reaching the Old City from Downtown. The Saen Saeb Express boats run from Saphan Phanfa Lela to Pratunam, and beyond if you transfer.

10 Khlong Bangkok Yai

Popular with tour boats, this canal passes several temples, including Wat Kalayanamit *(see p98)*, which has a huge Buddha image, and Wat Pak Nam, famous for its amulets. Many boats also stop at a snake farm and the floating market along Khlong Dao Khanong.

9 Chao Phraya – River of Kings

Without the Chao Phraya River **(below)**, there would be no Bangkok. Named for the founder of the Chakri dynasty, Chao Phraya Chakri *(see p40)*, the river has always been the lifeblood of the nation, providing an aquatic highway for a range of boats.

RIDING THE CHAO PHRAYA EXPRESS

River buses are a great way to see the Chao Phraya and beat the traffic. The central section from Sathorn (Central) pier upstream to Phra Athit takes around 30 minutes, passing by several sights, such as the Church of Santa Cruz *(see p98)*, Wat Arun, Wat Phra Kaeo *(see pp12–15)*, and Wat Rakhang *(see p98)*. The website www.chaophraya expressboat.com has more information.

TOP 10 ⭐ Dusit Park

Sometimes referred to as the New Royal City, Dusit is home to several royal residences and government offices. Dusit Park was created by Rama V in an attempt to emulate parks that he had seen on visits to Europe. The green and shady paths are a pleasure to walk along, with many interesting sights on offer.

4 Ancient Textile Museum

The highlights of this museum include a range of fabrics favored by the court of Rama V, such as rich Shanghai brocade silk, gold brocade cloth, and satin.

1 Abhisek Dusit Throne Hall/ SUPPORT Museum

This building **(above)** blends Victorian, Islamic, and Thai styles, with some timber latticework around the entrance. Inside, the SUPPORT Museum features traditional crafts. The hall is used for royal receptions.

2 Old Clock Museum

The splendid array of clocks on display at this museum (table, wall, and grandfather varieties all feature) were commissioned or acquired by Thailand's kings Rama V and Rama IX on their trips to Europe.

5 Dusit Zoo

Housing over 300 reptiles, 1,000 birds, and 300 mammals, this is one of Asia's better zoos, and Thailand's biggest. Originally Rama V's private botanical gardens, it has lawns, lakes, and glades, as well as a few modest rides for small children.

3 Royal Elephant Museum

The former stables of the king's white elephants house this fascinating museum **(left)**, which features pachyderm paraphernalia such as howdahs, sacred ropes, and mahouts' amulets. There are photos of the king's white elephants, as well as a model of a current favorite.

Map of Dusit Park

7 Vimanmek Palace

Possibly the world's largest teak building **(below)**, this palace was the home of Rama V *(see p40)* in the early 20th century and contains a huge collection of royal artifacts. Visitors can join a guided tour to see 30 of its 72 rooms.

HM KING BHUMIBOL ADULYADEJ (1927–2016)

The ninth king of the Chakri dynasty *(see pp40–41)*, Rama IX reigned for 70 years, from 1946 until his death in 2016. The Thai people's deep love for their king – bordering on worship – was due to his common touch and selfless devotion to the country's welfare. The outpouring of grief across Thailand at his death was profound.

6 Ananta Samakhom Throne Hall

Built in Renaissance style, this marble hall **(below)**, the largest building in Dusit Park, showcases Thai masterpieces at the Arts of the Kingdom exhibition.

8 Royal Plaza

On the south side of Dusit Park is this large open area dominated by an equestrian statue of Rama V, who designed the park. It was here that the People's Party staged the 1932 bloodless revolution *(see p40)*.

9 Lakeside Pavilion

Overlooking a tranquil stretch of water is a delightful lakeside pavilion. Decorated with ornate carvings, it is occasionally used for performances of Thai dancing.

10 Photographic Museum

Rama IX was a keen photographer, and examples of his work, including photos of the royal family, are exhibited at this museum.

NEED TO KNOW

MAP E1 ▪ Bus 56 and 70

Ananta Samakhom Throne Hall: open 10am–4pm daily; adm B150 (sarong for modesty B50); 02 283 9411 or 02 283 9185; www.artsofthe kingdom.com

Vimanmek Palace, Abhisek Dusit Throne Hall/Support Museum, Old Clock Museum, Royal Elephant Museum, Ancient

Textile Museum & Photographic Museum: closed for renovation. Call 02 628 6300 or visit www.vimanmek.com for details.

▪ Dress modestly: no shorts, short skirts, or sleeveless shirts.

▪ There is a café selling drinks and snacks at the entrance to Vimanmek Palace, but it is a good idea to carry a bottle of water with you.

Following pages Wat Pho's elaborate Scripture Hall

TOP 10 ⭐ Damnoen Saduak Floating Market

Today, the many waterways of Bangkok's once-extensive canal network have been filled in to make new roads, but the image of floating vendors in traditional dress remains quintessentially Thai. As a result, vendors and tourists alike descend on Damnoen Saduak each morning to re-enact scenes from an idealized past. Visitors can explore the canals, take pictures, and shop for souvenirs.

5 Ton Kem Market

What is referred to as Damnoen Saduak Floating Market is actually three separate markets, the biggest being Ton Kem Market on Khlong Damnoen Saduak **(below)**. This market is very popular with both tour groups and vendors, so the canal often gets jammed with boats.

1 Fruits

Many of the *sampans* (simple, square-ended rowing boats) on the canals here sell freshly picked pomelos, bananas, rose apples, and jackfruit **(above)**.

2 Bridge

There are plenty of opportunities for taking pictures while exploring by boat, but the classic view of the floating market, busy with boats, is from the bridge at Ton Kem market.

3 Fruit Orchards

To add variety to a visit to the floating market, many tour groups include a visit to an orchard to sample ripe fruit. Some orchards also keep harmless pythons, which tourists can drape round their necks for a souvenir photo.

OTHER FLOATING MARKETS

Damnoen Saduak gets the lion's share of visitors to floating markets, but there are other locations in and around Bangkok where similar markets operate, if only once a week. These include Amphawa, Tha Kha, Lam Phya, Don Wai, Wat Sai, and Taling Chan. The last two are near the center of Bangkok, but are exclusively for tourists.

4 Boat Noodles

It is a minor miracle that cooks can prepare a tasty bowl of *gooaydteeo rua* (boat noodles), in a small boat and serve it without spilling a drop **(below)**. These are so popular that noodle shops often display their dishes in a boat.

8 Boats
Most vendors paddle around in *sampans*, which are easily maneuvered and ideal for displaying goods for sale **(left)**. The tourists, however, are propelled around the canals in longtail boats. These boats can be noisy but offer protection from the elements and can cover a big area in a short time.

9 Boat Vendors
The *sampans* that the vendors paddle along the canals provide no protection from the elements, so most vendors wear a *ngob* – a traditional hat that ingeniously allows for ventilation. Many also wear a type of collarless denim shirt typical in rural Thailand.

6 Hia Kui Market
A short way south of Ton Kem, Hia Kui market has a more authentic feel to it. The banks of the canal are dotted with souvenir shops where some group tours stop for mementos.

7 Khun Pitak Market
On a smaller canal south of Hia Kui, Khun Pitak is the least crowded of the three markets, but it is still a bustling place early in the morning when locals buy fresh produce and spices.

10 Souvenirs
With busloads of tourists arriving in Damnoen Saduak every morning, many locals operate souvenir stalls on the banks of the canals, selling traditional hats **(above)**, silk purses, carved soaps, and, of course, colorful postcards of the market.

NEED TO KNOW

MAP S2 ▪ 62 miles (100 km) SW of Bangkok ▪ (03) 224 1204 ▪ AC bus 78 from Bangkok's Southern Bus Terminal

▪ To enjoy the market before busloads of tourists arrive (usually around 9–10am), it is necessary to stay overnight in a local guesthouse and get out on the canals in the early morning.

▪ Most guided tours include refreshments, but there are a large number of vendors selling food and drink for independent travelers.

🔟 ⭐ Chatuchak Weekend Market

Chatuchak Market, held every Saturday and Sunday, is the biggest market in Thailand. An estimated quarter of a million people visit this veritable shopaholic's paradise each day. The vast site has more than 15,000 stalls, but products are grouped by theme into a series of numbered sections, making it easy to find specific items.

① Home Decor

Items to beautify your home **(left)** can be found in sections 2 to 7. If you wish to buy bulky items, you can ship them home via a number of shipping companies located in the market.

② Crafts

Thailand is renowned all over the world for its handicrafts, including woodcarvings, basketware, lacquer-ware, ceramics, silk, silverware, and musical instruments. Such items can be found in section 8 of the market, where, with a little bit of luck, all the gifts you may need for friends and family can be bought in one go.

③ Plants

In this section of the market you can pick up a young fruit tree or a rose bush, a sweet-smelling jasmine plant, or a delicate orchid. They also sell fertilizer, flower pots, and gardening tools.

④ Chatuchak Park

If you need a break from the crowds, head to the adjacent Chatuchak Park **(below)**, just north of the market. Running the length of the park is an artificial lake. Also in the park is J. J. Green, a bohemian night market selling secondhand gear.

NEED TO KNOW

MAP T5 ■ Thanon Phaholyothin ■ Skytrain Mo Chit, Subway Chatuchak Park or Kampaeng Phet ■ www.chatuchak.org

Open 6am–6pm Sat & Sun

....

■ Go to Chatuchak in the morning to avoid the worst of the heat. Bargaining is expected, and some vendors will reduce their initial prices by half.

■ Simple maps are handed out free but serious shoppers should pick up Nancy Chandler's map of Bangkok, available at many bookstores and hotels.

■ To eat and drink in air-conditioned comfort, head for the Dream Section, where there are several smart restaurants.

7 Central Clock Tower

The tall clock tower **(left)** in the heart of the market is a useful landmark because it is visible from many areas. If you get lost, head for this clock tower, from where it should be easier to find your way.

ENDANGERED SPECIES

Unfortunately, Thailand is a major conduit for the sale of endangered species coming from neighboring countries. Several raids on dealers in Chatuchak Weekend Market have revealed animals being kept in awful conditions, and while casual visitors are never likely to see them, this illegal trade still continues out of sight.

10 Antiques

Located in section 26 of the market, antiques on sale include furniture, paintings, Buddha images **(left)**, lamps, jewelry, clocks, and carvings. However, take extra care when considering a purchase: Thai craftsmen are highly skilled in creating fakes, and all genuine antiques will need the appropriate documentation for customs clearance.

5 Books

Bibliophiles will love section 1, which has remaindered art books stacked beside collectible first editions and back issues of magazines. It is best visited last as the weight of purchases may discourage farther exploration of the market.

6 Food and Drink Stalls

More than 400 food and drink stalls are scattered throughout the market. Many of these stalls specialize in only one expertly cooked dish, so snacking here can be a gourmet experience.

8 Artists

There is an excellent art market located in section 7. Here, visitors will find small studios producing good-value paintings as well as higher-end pieces of art. Artists can be viewed at work on original pieces, and it is also possible to commission reproductions.

9 Clothing and Accessories

The market houses around 5,000 stalls that sell either clothes or fabric **(right)**, as well as fashion accessories. Most of them are in sections 12, 14, 16, 18, and 20. With rock-bottom prices, these are some of the most popular and crowded sections of the market.

TOP 10 ⭐ Jim Thompson House

Jim Thompson, an American businessman who came to Bangkok in 1945, is credited with having revived the Thai art of silk weaving. His traditional Thai house contains a fantastic selection of Southeast Asian antiques, paintings, and sculptures. Surrounded by a lush garden, the compound consists of five other teak houses on stilts that also showcase part of Thompson's collection.

4 Dining Room
Like the master bedroom, the dining room also enjoys lovely views of the garden. The room features several items of Ming porcelain as well as some fine paintings. The dining table, which consists of two mahjong tables put together, is laid out for a meal as it might have been during the days of Jim Thompson.

1 Drawing Room
This large and airy room looks out onto a terrace and is decorated in orange and red colors **(above)**. It houses a 14th-century sandstone head of the Buddha and wooden carvings of Burmese figures set in illuminated alcoves.

2 Jataka Paintings
Near the entrance of the house are scenes from the *Jataka Tales*, which depict the incarnations of the Buddha. The panels were painted in the early 1800s.

5 Spirit House
Located near the canal, the spirit house **(left)** generally has offerings of flowers and incense to appease the spirit of the land on which the house stands.

JIM THOMPSON'S DISAPPEARANCE

On Easter Day, 1967, Jim Thompson went out walking in the Cameron Highlands in Malaysia. He was never seen again. His former role in the Office of Strategic Services (OSS), a predecessor of the CIA, fueled suspicion that he was abducted by Vietnamese communists, though others suspect he was hit by a truck and that the driver buried the remains.

3 Master Bedroom
With a great view over the garden, this room is filled with sculptures, paintings of the *Jataka Tales*, and photographs of Jim Thompson.

6 The Garden
Surrounding the house is a garden with cooling pools and dense tropical vegetation **(below)** including flowers, banana plants, and palm trees.

8 Ban Khrua Silk Weavers

Thompson chose this location beside Khlong Saen Saeb because a silk weavers' community **(left)** lived at Ban Khrua, on the opposite bank. This made it easy for him to oversee their work.

9 Dvaravati Buddha Torso

Probably the most significant example of early Asian art at the complex, this headless Buddha torso, made of limestone during the Dvaravati period (7th–8th centuries), was found in Lopburi Province. The statue is on display in the garden that surrounds the house.

7 Traditional Teak Houses

The roofs of these six traditional stilted houses are steeply pitched for ventilation, and the walls lean inward to create a sense of height.

10 Burmese Carvings

These intricate carvings display a high level of artistic ability. Jim Thompson's extensive collection of wooden figures includes images of *nats* **(below)**, animist spirits that were incorporated into Buddhism when it developed in Myanmar.

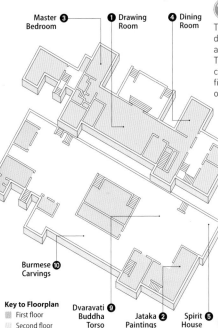

Master Bedroom **3** Drawing Room **1** Dining Room **4**

Burmese Carvings **10**

Key to Floorplan
■ First floor
▨ Second floor

Dvaravati Buddha Torso **9** Jataka Paintings **2** Spirit House **5**

NEED TO KNOW

MAP P2 ■ 6 Soi Kasem San 2, Rama 1 Road ■ 02 216 7368 ■ Skytrain National Stadium ■ www.jimthompson house.com

Open 9am–6pm daily
Adm: B150

■ Ignore any touts hanging around the house who tell you it is closed; they just want to take you shopping elsewhere so they can get a commission.

■ The branch of Jim Thompson Silk, located on the grounds, sells small souvenir items such as ties and purses, while the Jim Thompson Center for the Arts upstairs hosts fascinating temporary exhibitions.

■ The café (open 11am–5pm), and the wine bar and restaurant (open 7–11pm) offer repose next to a tranquil pond.

TOP 10 ⭐ Wat Arun

Wat Arun is named for Aruna, the Indian god of dawn, because King Taksin arrived here at sunrise on an October day in 1767 to establish Thonburi as Siam's new capital. With its prominent *prangs* (towers), the temple shows a strong Khmer influence. All the *prangs* are ornamentally encrusted with colorful broken porcelain.

NEED TO KNOW

MAP B5 ■ 34 Arun Amarin Road ■ 02 891 2185 ■ Cross-river ferry from Tha Tien Pier ■ www.watarun.org

Open 8:30am–6pm daily

Adm: B100

■ Due to ongoing renovations, it may not be possible to climb the stupa. However, the Wat Arun temple remains open to visitors.

■ Although strolling food and drink vendors do occasionally look for business at the temple, there is no permanent café here, so it's always best to carry a bottle of water with you around the complex.

■ If you visit in the late afternoon, in time to enjoy views of the temple at sunset, you can pause for refreshment at one of the cafés on the east bank of the river.

1 Stairs on Central Prang

The steep stairs up the central *prang* represent the difficulties humans face when trying to attain enlightenment. They lead up to a terrace with a view, but the upper stairway is often closed.

2 Chinese Guards

Steps lead up to the first terrace, and each set is guarded by Chinese figures that may have arrived as ballast on ships. There are also statues of many mythical creatures on the terrace.

3 River View

It may be called the Temple of Dawn, but the best view of Wat Arun is at sunset from the east bank of the river. There are cafés and restaurants around Tha Tien from where you can watch the sun slip down behind the soaring *prang* (below).

4 Central Prang

The central *prang* (above) was extended to its current height of 266 ft (81 m) by Rama III (r. 1824–51). It represents Mount Meru, the abode of the gods in Hindu-Buddhist cosmology. It is topped with a thunder-bolt, the weapon of the god Indra, who is also shown riding the three-headed elephant Erawan in niches on the *prang*.

5 Ceramic Details
The colorful ceramics **(above)** that cover the *prang* are an early form of recycling. In the 1800s, Chinese trading ships carried broken porcelain as ballast. When offloaded, it was used as decoration.

THE RISE AND FALL OF KING TAKSIN

Taksin the Great (r.1768–82) became one of Siam's most successful warrior kings. He waged wars with Cambodia, Laos, and the Malays, and by the 1770s he had expanded Siam to its largest-ever extent. Ousted in a coup, he was executed by being clubbed to death in a velvet sack so that royal blood would not touch the ground.

6 Kinnari
Tucked away in small coves on the second level of the central *prang* are *kinnaris*, creatures that are half-bird, half-woman. *Kinnaris* are just one of the many Thai mythical creatures (see p15) depicted at the temple.

8 The Bot
The Buddha image in the *bot* (ordination hall) was apparently molded by Rama II (r.1809–24) himself, and his ashes are buried in the base of the statue **(left)**. The murals were created during the reign of Rama V (see p40).

10 Symbolic Levels
The central *prang* has three symbolic levels. The base stands for *Traiphum*, all realms of existence in the Buddhist universe; the middle, *Tavatimsa*, where desires are gratified; the top, *Devaphum*, six heavens within seven realms of happiness.

7 Decoration of Minor Prangs
Representing the four great seas, these smaller *prangs* are supported by demons and monkeys. Each has a niche with a statue of Phra Pai, the god of wind, on a white horse.

9 Mondop
Between each of the four-cornered *prang* is a *mondop* (altar) **(right)**. Each holds a Buddha statue at key stages of his life – birth (north), meditation (east), preaching (south), and entering Nirvana (west).

TOP 10 ⭐ Ayutthaya

From the 14th century, Ayutthaya was the capital of an independent kingdom until the city was sacked by the Burmese in 1767. It was never restored as a capital city. Today, Ayutthaya is a UNESCO World Heritage Site, and its ruins give a sense of the city's former size and glory as well as offering an insight into Thailand's cultural heritage.

2 Wat Thammikarat
One of the park's most atmospheric temples has the ruins of an octagonal *chedi* (stupa), a *wihan*, and a fearsome *singha* (see p15) (left).

3 Ayutthaya Historical Study Center
This center attempts to depict the city's history and trading relations, with models of ships, houses, and other historical objects. It also houses a model of Wat Phra Si Sanphet, a once great temple that has been reduced to ruins.

1 Wihan Phra Mongkhon Bophit
This *wihan* (assembly hall) was built in the 1950s to shelter a very large bronze Buddha image that dates back to the 15th century.

4 Wat Phra Mahathat
An important temple during Ayutthaya's heyday, it remains one of the most evocative of all the city's sights (left), with smaller *prangs* (towers) leaning at precarious angles and a Buddha head encased by the roots of a banyan tree.

NEED TO KNOW

MAP T1 ■ 53 miles (85 km) N of Bangkok

Chao Sam Phraya National Museum: open 9am–4pm, Wed–Sun; adm B150

Ayutthaya Historical Study Center: open 9am–4:30pm Mon–Fri and 9am–5pm Sat–Sun; adm B100

■ Most temples are open 8am–6pm daily, and entrance usually costs B50 (some temples are free).

■ Some tour agencies include a boat trip either to or from Ayutthaya, the ideal way to approach the historic city.

■ The best way to get around is by bike, though many opt for tuk tuks or an air-conditioned minibus.

■ Malakor, in front of Wat Ratchaburuna, serves Thai and Western dishes.

5 **Chao Sam Phraya National Museum**

Most of Ayutthaya's precious artifacts, including gold Buddha images, were either taken by the invading Burmese or looters. A few remaining items are on show here **(right)**.

6 **Wat Phra Si Sanphet**

Once Ayutthaya's most glorious temple, all that is left of Wat Phra Si Sanphet **(below)** today, are three Sri Lankan-style *chedis* alongside the ruins of the royal palace. The *chedis* contain ashes of Ayutthayan kings and are the park's highlight.

A SHORT HISTORY OF AYUTTHAYA

Ayutthaya was founded by King Ramathibodi I in 1350. Over the next four centuries, the kingdom came to dominate the region now known as Thailand, apart from in the north (where the Kingdom of Lanna maintained its independence). Traders from Europe returned home with tales of a highly organized and sophisticated society. The kingdom's end was as sudden as its beginning, and its capital was completely abandoned after being sacked by the Burmese in 1767.

10 **Wat Ratchaburuna**

Next door to Wat Phra Mahathat, this temple was built in 1424 by King Borommaracha II, and its main structure is a Khmer-style *prang*. In 1957, the crypt beneath the *prang* was opened by robbers, who made off with a horde of gold artifacts. The few items they did not take are now on display in the Chao Sam Phraya National Museum. The crypt can be reached by a steep staircase, where there are beautiful frescoes.

Map of Ayutthaya

8 **Wang Luang**

Constructed in the 15th century by King Borommatrailokanat *(see p37)*, this royal palace had enough stable space for over 100 elephants. It was razed to the ground by the Burmese and only the foundations remain.

7 **Wat Phra Ram**

Wat Phra Ram is one of Ayutthaya's oldest temples. Originally built in 1369, the main *prang*, decorated with Buddha images and mythical creatures like *nagas* and *garudas* (*see p15*), was added during the 15th century.

9 **Wat Lokaya Sutharam**

The highlight of this temple is a huge, white-washed Reclining Buddha **(below)**, exposed to the elements. Pillars around it once supported a wooden hall that sheltered the image.

Sights In and Around Ayutthaya

① Bang Pa-In
15 miles (24 km) S of Ayutthaya ■ **Open 8am–4pm daily** ■ **Adm**

Included on many tours of Ayutthaya, this former royal summer retreat is an eclectic mix of Thai and Western architectural styles. The Aisawan Thipphaya-at pavilion that sits on a lake is its most photographed building.

② Wat Yai Chai Mongkol
1 mile (2 km) E of Ayutthaya ■ **Open 8am–5pm daily** ■ **Adm**

Aisawan Thipphaya-at pavilion at Bang Pa-In

The main features of this temple include a huge *chedi* (stupa) erected by King Naresuan, a host of saffron-robed, laterite Buddha images that surround it, and a large Reclining Buddha set in a corner of the temple grounds.

③ Wat Phanan Choeng
S of Ayutthaya ■ **Open 8am–5pm daily** ■ **Adm**

Particularly popular with Chinese worshippers because of a shrine to a Chinese princess, this temple dates back to the 14th century. Its centerpiece is a 62-ft- (19-m-) tall, seated bronze image of Phra Chao Phanan Choeng.

④ Lopburi
44 miles (70 km) N of Ayutthaya

One of Thailand's oldest towns, Lopburi was an important center of Dvaravati culture from the 6th century onwards. Both King Narai the Great and Rama IV *(see p40)* used it as a second capital, and Narai's palace is well worth a visit.

⑤ Chantarakasem Palace Museum
NE corner of Ayutthaya ■ **Open 8:30am–4:30pm Wed–Sun** ■ **Adm**

Ayutthaya's oldest museum displays a throne platform that belonged to Rama IV, some beautiful ceramics and Buddha images, and a collection of cannons and muskets.

⑥ Wat Na Phra Mane
N of Ayutthaya ■ **Open 8am–5pm Mon–Fri, 8am–6pm Sat–Sun** ■ **Adm**

This temple was less badly damaged than most by the invading Burmese and is therefore one of the most interesting to explore. Inside is a large *bot* (ordination hall), which displays some fine architectural features, and a small *wihan* (assembly hall) with a rare Dvaravati stone Buddha.

Statue in Wat Phanan Choeng

7 Wat Phu Khao Thong
1 mile (2 km) NW of Ayutthaya

Also known as the Golden Mount, this temple's main feature is its *chedi*. It is possible to climb part of the way up the structure to get a panoramic view of the rice fields.

8 Wat Puthaisawan
S of Ayutthaya

Located across the river from central Ayutthaya, the temple has a restored 14th-century *prang* (tower), which is surrounded by cloisters that are packed with Buddha images.

9 Wat Chai Wattanaram
W of Ayutthaya

Built in the 17th century and restored in the late 20th century, Wat Chai Wattanaram is modeled on Angkor Wat in Cambodia, with a central *prang* surrounded by eight smaller ones.

10 St. Joseph's Cathedral
W of Ayutthaya

A cathedral was built here in the 17th century to accommodate the needs of foreign merchants, who were not permitted to enter the city center except by invitation. The cathedral was renovated in the 19th century and is still functional.

Interior of St. Joseph's Cathedral

KING NARAI THE GREAT (R.1656–88)

Narai is best remembered for his warming of diplomatic relations with Western countries, his sending of missions to European courts, and his selection of a foreigner, Constantine Phaulkon, as his principal advisor. It was from reports by European merchants of this era that Ayutthaya became known in the west for its richness and splendor. Phaulkon encouraged Narai to balance Dutch interests in the kingdom by inviting a French delegation to visit. However, many Siamese suspected, quite correctly as it turned out, that the French mission's main objective was to convert the king to Christianity, and on Narai's death French officials and troops were banished from Ayutthaya.

King Narai the Great was a usurper, like most kings of Ayutthaya, and he deposed his uncle, Si Suthammaracha, to take the throne.

TOP 10
KINGS OF AYUTTHAYA

1 **Ramathibodi** (r.1351–69)

2 **Borommaracha I** (r.1370–88)

3 **Borommaracha II** (r.1424–48)

4 **Borommatrailokanat** (r.1448–88)

5 **Ramathibodi II** (r.1491–1529)

6 **Naresuan** (r.1590–1605)

7 **Prasat Thong** (r.1629–56)

8 **Narai** (r.1656–88)

9 **Phra Phetracha** (r.1688–1703)

10 **Phumintharacha** (r.1758–67)

The Top 10
of Everything

The bustling interior of Central World
shopping mall

🔟 Moments in History

① 1767: Ayutthaya Overrun by the Burmese

After 400 years of being one of Asia's most powerful empires, the Kingdom of Ayutthaya (see pp34–7) was invaded by Burmese troops in 1767. Though the Burmese were expelled within a year, Ayutthaya was deemed unsafe as a capital and General Taksin chose Thonburi as the new capital of Siam (now Thailand).

② 1782: Bangkok Founded

Just 15 years later, a rebellion against Taksin's autocratic rule led to his demise. He was succeeded by General Chao Phraya Chakri who established the Chakri dynasty and acquired the official title of Rama I. On assuming the throne, his first action was to move the capital east across the river to Bangkok.

③ 1851: Rama IV Crowned

After 27 years as a monk, King Mongkut acceded to the throne to become Rama IV of the Chakri dynasty. Thais regard him as the man who began to modernize Siam, particularly through treaties that opened the country to trade with the West.

④ 1868: Rama V Crowned

Chulalongkorn, son of Rama IV, succeeded his father as Rama V of the Chakri Dynasty when he was only 15 years old. He ruled for over 40 years and is credited with keeping Siam free

Rama V, King of Siam (r.1868–1910)

from the clutches of colonial powers such as England and France, which were carving up Southeast Asia at the time.

⑤ 1893: First Railroad Line

Rama V carried on his father's programme of modernization, and in 1893 the country's first railroad line opened, stretching just 14 miles (22 km) to Pak Nam. The line was later extended to the south, north, and northeast of the country.

Rama IV, crowned in 1851

⑥ 1932: End to Absolute Monarchy

The absolute power of the Siamese monarchy was ended by a bloodless coup in 1932. It brought the military to power, setting the stage for the string of coups and counter-coups that dominated the politics of Thailand for the rest of the century.

7 1946: Rama IX Ascends the Throne

After the death of his brother King Mahidol, who was shot in the head while in bed, King Bhumibol Adulyadej took the throne as Rama IX. He reigned for 70 years, until his death in 2016.

8 1992: Military Government Ousted

Thais demonstrated publicly their displeasure following a military coup in 1992. After the army gunned down many citizens on the streets of Bangkok, Rama IX intervened, resulting in the self-proclaimed Prime Minister, General Suchinda Kraprayoon, making a hasty exit and democracy being restored.

The military coup of 1992

9 2006: Thaksin Ousted

Thailand's self-styled "CEO leader" Thaksin Shinawatra swept to power in 2001 as head of the Thai Rak Thai party, inspiring people with his business acumen. However, he was ousted for corruption in a military coup in September 2006.

10 2011: Thailand's First Female Prime Minister

Thaksin's sister Yingluck was elected Thailand's first female Prime Minister, widely viewed as a proxy for her brother. She was deposed in a 2014 coup by General Prayut Chan-o-cha, who went on to oversee the succession of Rama X, King Vajiralongkorn, in 2016.

TOP 10 FAMOUS THAIS

Anand Panyarachun

1 Chang and Eng Bunker
Born near Bangkok, the original Siamese Twins (1811–74) settled in the USA, married, and fathered 22 children. They died within hours of each other.

2 Plaek Pibulsonggram
Prime Minister and military dictator for around 15 years, Pibulsonggram changed the country's name from Siam to Thailand in 1939.

3 Kukrit Pramoj
Thailand's 13th Prime Minister (1975–6) was honored in 1985 as National Artist for his literary works.

4 Prem Tinsulanonda
The country's Prime Minister from 1980–88, Tinsulanonda was one of the closest advisors to King Rama IX.

5 Anand Panyarachun
Serving twice as Prime Minister in the early 1990s, Panyarachun made overdue reforms to the Thai constitution in 1996.

6 Khaosai Galaxy
The "Thai Tyson," Khaosai was WBA Super Flyweight champion from 1984 to 1992, defending his title 19 times.

7 Apsara Hongsakula
Crowned Miss Universe in 1965, this beauty queen was the first of three Thai women to win the accolade.

8 Thongchai McIntyre
Known as "Bird," Thailand's biggest pop idol also has a film and TV acting career.

9 Thaksin Shinawatra
This former police officer and telecoms billionaire fronts the populist political movement known as the Red Shirts.

10 Chalermchai Kositpipat
The Buddhism-inspired works of Thailand's greatest contemporary artist include an entire temple in Chiang Rai.

TOP 10 Museums and Art Galleries

1 National Museum

An accurate overview of the evolution of Thai culture is laid out in the National Museum *(see pp16–17)* through exquisite Sukhothai, Ayutthaya, Rattanakosin, and Lanna artifacts. Don't miss the Ramkhamhaeng stone, bearing the oldest known inscription using the Thai alphabet, the Royal Funeral Chariots Gallery, and the Buddhaisawan Chapel.

2 Royal Barge Museum

Housed in a dry-dock ware-house, this museum features eight gleaming barges, each nearly 165 ft (50 m) long, that are used only for special royal events. The biggest and most important barge, *Suphannahongse*, carries the king himself *(see p96)*.

3 National Gallery

Both traditional and contemporary Thai art are featured at this gallery *(see p72)*. There are also many temporary exhibitions. Temple banners are displayed in the section upstairs, and there is an art market in the courtyard each weekend.

Royal Barge Museum

4 Museum of Contemporary Art

MAP T5 ■ Vibhavadi Rangsit Road, Chatuchak ■ 02 016 5666 ■ Open 10am–5pm Tue–Fri, 11am–6pm Sat & Sun ■ Adm ■ www. moca.bangkok.com

This modernist five-story museum is the pride of Thai contemporary artists, with more than 800 pieces on permanent display. Entire galleries are dedicated to the works of Thailand's most famous artists, including Chalermchai Kositpipat and Tawan Dachanee.

5 H Gallery

MAP N6 ■ 201 Sathorn Soi 12 ■ 085 021 5508 ■ Open 10am–6pm Wed–Mon ■ www.hgallery bkk.com

Situated in a colonial building on Silom Road, H Gallery mainly exhibits abstract works by contemporary Asian artists such as Cambodian artist Sopheap Pich's sculptures.

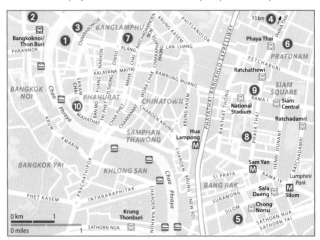

Traditional houses surrounded by lush greenery in Suan Pakkad

6 Suan Pakkad

A compound of traditional Thai houses, Suan Pakkad (see p86) is an excellent example of Thai architecture. The houses contain antique paintings, carvings, and a stunning display of masks used in *khon* (masked theater).

7 The Queen's Gallery

MAP D3 ▪ 101 Ratchadamnoen Klang Road ▪ 02 281 5361 ▪ Open 10am–7pm Thu–Tue ▪ Adm ▪ www.queengallery.org

Established in 2003 at the request of Queen Sirikit, this gallery occupies a massive 39,825 sq ft (3,700 sq m) of exhibition space. The Queen wanted to showcase leading examples of Thai visual art. The gallery's shop stocks an interesting range of glossy art books and T-shirts featuring contemporary art.

8 The Art Center

MAP P3 ▪ Center of Academic Resources Building, Seventh Floor, Chulalongkorn University, Phaya Thai Road ▪ 02 218 2965 ▪ Open 9am–7pm Mon–Fri, 9am–4pm Sat ▪ www.omega.car.chula.ac.th/art/en

One of two galleries on the campus grounds near Siam Square at Bangkok's prestigious Chulalongkorn University, The Art Center features work by professors from the university as well as by established Thai and international artists. The gallery is known for experimentation and its interactive installations.

9 Bangkok Art & Culture Centre

Housing several galleries of contemporary art on its upper floors, connected by spiralling ramps like New York's Guggenheim Museum, the prestigious Bangkok Art & Culture Centre (see p62) covers all media, from the visual arts to music and design. There's usually an interesting exhibition on here, as well as a performance in one of the performance spaces.

10 Museum of Siam

Highly imaginative, this interactive museum covers the history, art, culture and traditions of Thailand from the distant past to the present with audio-visual and traditional displays. It's a museum that kids will really love (see p72).

Interior of the Museum of Siam

🔟 Buddhist Temples

① Wat Bowoniwet
Built in 1826, this temple has gained significance for being the place where Thai kings are ordained and as one of the main bases of Buddhism in Thailand. The murals inside feature some unusual themes, such as horse racing in England and Dutch windmills *(see p72)*.

Wat Suthat's bronze Buddha

② Wat Suthat
One of the most important temples in Thailand, Wat Suthat was built in the early 1800s to house the 26-ft- (8-m-) tall bronze Buddha image from Sukhothai, which sits in the *wihan*, surrounded by murals. The galleries around the *wihan* hold over 150 Buddha images. The towering Sao Ching Cha, or Giant Swing, once used in a Brahmin ceremony, stands in front of the temple *(see p71)*.

③ Wat Traimit
This gleamingly rebuilt temple located in Chinatown is firmly fixed on the tourist trail because of the Golden Buddha, a 10-ft- (3-m-) high Sukhothai-style image made of solid gold *(see p76)*.

④ Wat Suwannaram
On the Bangkok Noi canal in Thonburi, near the Royal Barges museum, this Ayutthaya-style temple was built during the reign of King Taksin. Step into the main building of the temple to see some of best temple murals in the country, including depictions of Westerners from the Ayutthaya era *(see p98)*.

⑤ Wat Mahathat
MAP B3 ▪ Mahathat Road ▪ (02) 221 5999 ▪ Open 7am–8pm daily
Prince Mongkut was a monk in Wat Mahathat for 12 years before he became Rama IV *(see p40)*. Mahachulalongkorn Buddhist University and a meditation center are housed in the temple complex.

⑥ Wat Saket and the Golden Mount
Built by Rama I in the late 1700s, this temple has some excellent murals and a peaceful atmosphere. The main attraction, though, is the view of the Old City from the Golden Mount, a 250-ft (76-m) high man-made hill inside the temple *(see p70)*.

⑦ Wat Benjamabophit
MAP E2 ▪ Nakhon Pathom Road ▪ (02) 282 7413 ▪ Open 8am–5:30pm daily ▪ Adm
The last major temple built in Bangkok (between 1899 and 1911), this is commonly known to Western visitors as the Marble Temple because of its extraordinary Carrara marble *bot*. The ashes of Rama V are buried beneath the temple's golden Buddha image.

Wat Benjamabophit

Golden *chedi* at Wat Phra Kaeo

8 Wat Phra Kaeo

For many visitors, the highlight of their stay in Bangkok is a visit to Wat Phra Kaeo, to see beautiful examples of Buddhist art and architecture. It features a glittering array of *chedis*, libraries, mausoleums, and the small jadeite Buddha that is the nation's greatest treasure *(see pp12–15)*.

9 Wat Ratchabophit

MAP C4 ■ Fuang
Nakhon Road ■ 02 221
1888 ■ Open
5am–8pm daily;
bot: open
9–9:30am,
5:30–6pm daily

A blend of local and Western architecture, this temple was built in the late 19th century by Rama V *(see p40)*. Its 141-ft (43-m) *chedi* is surrounded by cloisters, into which are set a *wihan* and a *bot* designed like an Italian Gothic chapel.

Detail of Wat Ratchabophit

10 Wat Pho

Bangkok's biggest and oldest temple, Wat Pho's main attraction is its 150-ft- (46-m-) long Reclining Buddha. This *wat* is more typical of temples countrywide than Wat Phra Kaeo because it has resident monks who live in simple lodgings within the complex. It also runs a respected school of massage *(see pp18–19)*.

TOP 10 ELEMENTS OF A THAI TEMPLE COMPOUND

1 Wihan
The main assembly hall of a temple, where the head abbot gives sermons and people come to pray.

2 Bot
The ordination hall, which is usually smaller than the *wihan*. Highly decorated, it is off-limits to women.

3 Chedi
These dome-shaped religious monuments, or stupas, have relics sealed within their base.

4 Bodhi Tree
This tree *(Ficus religiosa)* symbolizes Enlightenment, as the Buddha is said to have been sitting beneath a Bodhi tree when he attained Nirvana.

5 Ho Trai
The library in each temple stores sacred texts and is often raised off the ground to avoid flood damage.

6 Guti
These are the monks' living quarters in a temple complex – sometimes a small, austere wooden room set on stilts.

7 Murals
Temple murals depict incidents from the life of the Buddha, and some record scenes of Thai daily life.

8 Buddha Images
Usually the most highly valued Buddha image is placed in the *wihan*. Other images may sit or stand in the *bot* or cloisters.

9 Monks
These are holy men who follow the Buddha's teachings and advise lay people on their problems.

10 Novices
Young men live as novices in the temple before being ordained as monks.

A Buddha's head in a Bodhi tree

🔟 Spas

① Banyan Tree Spa

MAP Q5 ▪ Banyan Tree Hotel, Sathorn Road ▪ 02 679 1052 ▪ Open 10am–10pm daily ▪ www.banyantreespa.com

Located on the 39th floor of the Banyan Tree Hotel, this deluxe spa has fantastic views and offers an extensive menu of services, including the 150-minute Royal Banyan package, comprising a herbal pouch massage, a face massage, and a herbal bath.

② Oriental Spa

MAP M5 ▪ Oriental Hotel ▪ 02 659 9000 extn. 7440 ▪ Open 8am–10pm daily ▪ www.mandarinoriental.com

This spa is an oasis of calm, combining ancient Asian healing philosophies with modern Western techniques. The traditional Thai teak building is the ideal place to unwind with a massage, floral mask facial, or Oriental mud wrap.

③ Anantara Siam Spa

MAP Q3 ▪ Anantara Siam Hotel, Ratchadamri Road ▪ 02 126 8866 ▪ Open 10am–10pm daily ▪ www.siam-bangkok.anantara.com

Each suite in this spa has a large Roman bathtub and is decorated in traditional Thai style. The treatments include a Japanese-style bamboo massage and specific therapies for men and those overcoming jet-lag.

Interior at Anantara Siam Spa

Chi, The Spa, at the Shangri-La

④ Chi, The Spa

MAP M6 ▪ Shangri-La Hotel ▪ 02 236 7777 ▪ Open 10am–10pm daily ▪ www.shangri-la.com/en

Based on the design of a Tibetan temple, this spa facility is nothing less than a sanctuary of tranquility. The wide array of treatments is designed to restore *chi* (a Chinese term that refers to the universal life force that governs well-being and personal vitality). Eleven spacious treatment rooms offer sweeping river views and are equipped with an infinity bath, a herbal steam shower, and relaxation and changing areas.

⑤ The Oasis Spa at Sukhumvit 51

MAP T6 ▪ 88 Sukhumvit Soi 51 ▪ 02 262 2122 ▪ Open 10am–10pm daily ▪ www.oasisspa.net

This day spa is set in lush tropical gardens and is tastefully decorated with teak furniture and cotton fabrics from Bali. The wide range of treatments on offer includes facials and massages, taken individually or as spa packages. Try the aloe and lavender body wrap or the Ayurvedic body massage.

6 The Grande Spa

MAP T6 ■ The Sheraton Grande Sukhumvit, 250 Sukhumvit Road ■ 02 649 8121 ■ Open 9am–11pm daily ■ www.sheratongrandesukhumvit.com

Located at the five-star Sheraton, this spa has an excellent reputation. Treatments combine the timeless wisdom of Thailand's healing arts with the very best of contemporary trends, and include facials, scrubs, wraps and massages.

7 The Oasis Spa

MAP T6 ■ 64 Sukhumvit Soi 31 ■ 02 262 2122 ■ Open 10am–10pm daily ■ www.oasisspa.net

This day spa facility is set in a huge garden which helps to create an aura of calm, with birds twittering in the trees outside the treatment rooms. Options provided by the spa include an "Oasis Four Hands Massage", in which two masseurs work in unison, and the "King of Oasis", which involves Thai and oil massages with hot compresses.

8 Treasure Spa

MAP T6 ■ 33 Thonglor Soi 13 ■ 02 391 7694 ■ Open 10am–10pm daily ■ www.treasurespa.com

This is another day spa set in a lush, tropical garden. It offers a dizzying array of treatments – massage, facial, body scrub, and body wrap, plus half-day packages. The body scrubs use tropical ingredients such as mango and lemongrass, while the massage employs an aromatic blend of essential oils.

9 I. Sawan Residential Spa and Club

MAP Q3 ■ Grand Hyatt Erawan, 494 Ratchadamri Road ■ 02 254 1234 ■ Open 9am–11pm daily ■ www.bangkok.grand.hyatt.com

This luxurious spa, set amid the Grand Hyatt Erawan's lovely roof gardens, offers an extensive range of treatments, each falling into one of four categories: Energy, Harmony, Purity, or Thai.

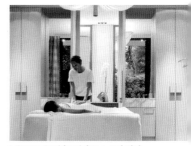

I. Sawan Residential Spa and Club

10 Health Land

MAP N6 ■ 120 N Sathorn Road ■ 02 637 8883 ■ Open 9am–11pm daily ■ www.healthlandspa.com

This chain of spas caters to those who want a good massage and other spa services in a clean private room at a reasonable price. Full spa treatments, including facials and body polishes are on offer, and the therapists are well trained.

📖10 Sport and Leisure

T'ai chi practice at Lumphini Park

1 Martial Arts

It is possible to study and practise all kinds of martial arts in Bangkok, from Thai boxing to tae kwon do, judo, or karate, though probably the most popular is t'ai chi. To join the city's inhabitants for an impromptu session of t'ai chi or aerobics, head along to Lumphini Park (see p86) at dawn or dusk.

2 Horse Racing

RTC: MAP F2; Phitsanulok Road; 02 280 0020–9; adm

There are a couple of race courses in Bangkok: the Royal Turf Club (RTC) in Dusit and the Royal Bangkok Sports Club (RBSC). Races are held on alternate Sundays at RBSC (see p88) and RTC. The minimum bet is B50. The Silom line of the Skytrain provides a view of the RBSC.

3 Golf

This game is very popular among visitors to Bangkok for a variety of reasons – courses are generally of a high international standard, with scenic landscaping, competitive equipment rental and green fees, and attentive and friendly service. There are several courses within easy reach of Bangkok.

4 Tennis

National Stadium: MAP N2; 154 Rama I Rd; 02 214 0120

A fashionable sport in Bangkok, it is best to play early in the morning or late in the afternoon to avoid the searing heat. Major hotels have private tennis courts; public courts are at the National Stadium and in Lumphini Park (see p86).

5 Takraw

Best described as volleyball played with the feet, takraw is visually exciting, with the players performing acrobatic feats to kick the ball over the net. Games are played in Sanam Luang (see p69), public parks, or any small open space in Bangkok.

6 Cycling

Cycling is really popular in Bangkok. In addition to rural routes at Bang Krajao (see p97), cyclists can ride in Lumphini Park (see p86) or on the bike lanes in the Old City. Bike-share kiosks and rentals abound.

7 Snooker

Since James Wattana joined the world rankings, snooker has become hugely popular in Thailand. There are thousands of clubs across the country, with hundreds of them in Bangkok. Tables are usually in excellent condition, cues are on hand, and hourly rates are reasonable.

The Royal Bangkok Sports Club golf course and race track

8 Bowling

For a fun afternoon or evening with friends, go bowling. It offers a sporting challenge without too much exertion. Most Bangkok shopping malls have a bowling alley on the top floor, some equipped with karaoke facilities and disco lighting.

9 Ice Skating

Sub Zero: MAP T6; Major Cineplex Sukhumvit; 02 391 1944; open noon–9pm Mon–Thu, noon–10pm Fri, 10am–10pm Sat & Sun; adm

Ice rinks are rarely on a visitor's itinerary on a tropical holiday but there are a few on the outskirts. Coaches are on hand to teach beginners.

A Thai boxing match in progress

10 Thai Boxing

Muay Thai (Thai boxing) has enjoyed an explosion of popularity, particularly with young Westerners, many of whom spend their holidays in Thailand practising the sport in camps. Less active visitors may attend bouts at the Ratchadamnoen Boxing Stadium *(see p51)*.

TOP 10 THAI SPORTING EVENTS

International Kite Festival

1 International Kite Festival
Hua Hin ▪ Mar (biennial)
There are individual and team events at this traditional festival and a range of unusual kites are on display.

2 Chiang Mai Cricket Sixes
Chiang Mai ▪ Apr
A fun event with occasional big names.

3 Koh Samui Regatta
Chaweng Beach ▪ May/Jun
A highlight of the Asian sailing circuit.

4 Phuket Marathon
Laguna Phuket Resort ▪ Jun
Thailand's biggest marathon attracts thousands of entries each year.

5 Tour of Thailand
Routes vary ▪ Nov
A bicycle road race of 16 stages that draws riders from around the world.

6 Longboat Races
Phimai & elsewhere ▪ Oct & Nov
Great to see out of the rainy season.

7 Six Red Snooker World Championship
Bangkok ▪ Sep
Fast-paced tournament that uses six reds rather than the usual fifteen.

8 Chula–Thammasat Football Match
Bangkok ▪ Jan
Held since 1934, this varsity match between two top universities features satirical parades and card stunts.

9 Laguna Phuket Triathlon
Laguna Phuket Resort ▪ Nov
A gruelling challenge for athletes in a sport that tests their swimming, cycling, and running skills.

10 King's Cup Regatta
Phuket ▪ Dec
Since its inception in 1987, this has become Asia's premier international sailing event, and it attracts huge crowds.

TOP 10 Entertainment Venues

A stage full of actors and dancers at the National Theatre

1 National Theatre
MAP B3 ■ Rachini Road ■ 02 224 1342 ■ Adm

Impressive productions of Thai classical drama such as *khon* (masked theater) with skilled actors and sumptuous costumes are staged at the National Theatre on the last Friday of every month. Modern Thai dramas and musical shows are also performed here.

2 Siam Niramit
MAP T5 ■ Ratchada Theater, 19 Tiam Ruammit Road ■ 02 649 9222 ■ Show 8pm daily ■ Adm ■ www.siamniramit.com

A cultural extravaganza designed for tourists, this show presents an idealized vision of ancient Siam using hi-tech special effects, lavish costumes, and a cast of hundreds.

3 Silom Village
MAP N5 ■ Silom Road ■ 02 635 6313 ■ Indoor show with set dinner 8:15–9pm daily ■ Adm ■ www. silomvillage.co.th

Thai dancers at a cultural show in Bangkok

Accompanied by dinner (served from 7:30pm), this show at the Ruen Thep hall in Silom Village features various forms of Thai dance. The standard of the performance and quality of the food make it a good choice for an evening's entertainment.

4 Tawandang German Brewery
Enjoy a wildly entertaining cabaret, featuring Thai as well as Western pop and folk music, ballet, hip-hop dancing, and magic shows at the Tawandang German Brewery. The huge dome of this vast all-round venue can host up to 1,600 revellers and it offers good food and great micro-brewed German beer (see p101).

5 Sala Chalermkrung Royal Theatre
MAP C5 ■ Charoen Krung Road ■ 02 222 0434 ■ Khon: 7:30pm Thu & Fri ■ www.salachalerm krung.com

Built in 1933 by Rama VII, this was Thailand's first theater to be built with the intention of screening "talking pictures." Today it is used for staging *khon* (masked theater) and for live performances by singers and musicians.

6 Thailand Cultural Centre

MAP T5 ▪ Ratchadaphisek Road ▪ 02 247 0028 ▪ www.culture.go.th

Bangkok's main center for the performing arts, this state-run facility is home to the Bangkok Symphony Orchestra. It also hosts the annual International Festival of Dance and Music. International artists also perform here during world tours, so check for upcoming events.

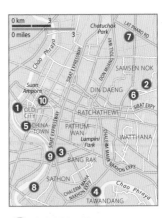

7 Playhouse Theater

MAP T5 ▪ Suan Lum Night Bazaar, 5 Ratchadapisek Road, Chom Phon ▪ 02 024 5522 ▪ Show 7pm, 8:20pm daily ▪ Adm ▪ www.playhousethailand.com

Performed at the Suan Lum Night Bazaar, the Playhouse ladyboy cabaret is an extravagant theater show featuring glamorous Thai dancers, elaborate stage sets, and a great selection of well-known songs from musicals.

8 Calypso Cabaret

Cabarets performed by transvestites are popular in Thailand. This famous show involves an entertaining cast of ladyboys looking absolutely sensational in sequins and stockings, lip-synching and dancing to pop songs, with well choreographed dance routines *(see p101)*.

A performer at Calypso Cabaret

9 Sala Rim Naam

MAP M5 ▪ Mandarin Oriental Hotel ▪ 02 437 3080 ▪ Lunch: noon–2:30pm daily; dinner: 7–10:30pm daily; show: 8:15pm daily ▪ www.mandarinoriental.com

This is a custom-built facility offering a show of traditional Thai dance and a gourmet dinner. Prices are above average, but the event is memorable.

The dining area at Sala Rim Naam

10 Ratchadamnoen Boxing Stadium

MAP E2 ▪ 1 Ratchadamnoen Nok Road ▪ 02 281 4205 ▪ Bouts: 6:30–11pm Mon, Wed, Thu; 5–8pm and 8:30pm–midnight Sun ▪ Adm

An evening of *muay Thai*, or Thai boxing *(see p49)* is great fun. You'll not only experience the thrill of the fight, but will also see how worked up the Thai spectators get. Add the strange pre-fight dances by the boxers to the accompaniment of wailing instruments, and you have a night of exotic Oriental fun.

Off the Beaten Path

① EmQuartier Tropical Garden

MAP T6 ■ Scala Building, 5th floor, EmQuartier Mall, Sukhumvit Road

No luxury goods are for sale in this part of EmQuartier mall – it's just an amazing rooftop garden with lavish displays of tropical plants, shaded resting spots, ponds, and a grassy meadow. The French designer, Patrick Blanc, added a rainforest chandelier as a finishing touch.

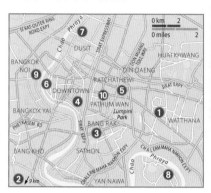

② Wat Hua Krabeu

MAP T2 ■ Bang Khun Tian ■ www.wathuakrabeu.com

This amazing Buddhist temple is the work of an eccentric monk who pays tribute to the water buffalo, Thailand's traditional draft animal, by collecting their skulls – he currently has around 10,000 of them. The temple is located on a canal, and a number of passing boats offer tours.

Buffalo skulls at Wat Hua Krabeu

③ Chao Mae Tubtim Shrine

The phallic architecture found here represents fertility and good fortune. Large stone penises stand amid the trees. Women hoping for a child come here to make offerings of incense, flowers, and wooden penises to the resident spirit. This is a peaceful spot by the Saen Saeb canal (see p88).

④ Chinatown's Soi Nana

MAP F5 ■ Between Charoen Krung and Luang roads, Chinatown

Not to be confused with the go-go-bar area of the same name on Sukhumvit Road, this residential neighborhood buzzes with chic cafés, art galleries, bars with live music, and small restaurants. Try the Tep Bar for innovative tunes and Thai food (see p81).

⑤ Sathorn Road, Sois 10–12

MAP M6

Japanese cuisine, vegetarian food and Western comfort food can be found in this cluster of chic independent restaurants on a tree-lined loop off Sathorn Road. With a range of hot nightspots located nearby (see p92), it's very popular with young professionals, both Thai and from the expat community.

⑥ Queen Sirikit Museum of Textiles

Often overlooked by visitors to the Grand Palace (it's on the right just after the main entrance), this superb museum displays a fine collection of textiles from throughout Asia, with an emphasis on royal attire and the renowned Thai silk. The building (formerly the Royal Treasury) gleams with white marble from Italy (see pp12–13).

Grounds of the Floral Culture Museum

7 Floral Culture Museum

MAP S5 ■ Soi 28 Samsen Rd, Dusit ■ 02 669 3633 ■ Open 10am–6pm Tue–Sun ■ Adm ■ www.floral museum.com

Located in a lovely teak house, this museum celebrates the role of flora in Thai culture, from religious to artistic perspectives. There are cut-flower displays and paintings inside and an extensive garden outside, along with an elegant tea salon.

8 Bang Krajao

Often called Bangkok's green lung, this protected enclave is on the west bank of the Chao Phraya River and is easy to reach by boat (from behind Wat Klong Toey Nok, among other piers). It's an ideal spot for cycling, with bikes available for rent, and there is also a good market here on weekends. The area is also gaining a reputation for its popular eco-resort *(see p117)*.

9 Museum of Forensic Medicine

MAP A3 ■ Siriraj Hospital, Thonburi ■ 02 419 7000 ■ Open 10am–5pm Wed–Mon ■ Adm ■ www.si.mahidol. ac.th

Its local nickname, "Museum of Death," sums up this fascinating place. Skeletons, embalmed bodies (including the remains of a notorious serial killer), and crime-scene evidence all make for a grisly yet informative visit. Other museums exploring medicine and local history can also be found on the hospital's grounds and are worth checking out while here.

Art Deco interior of Scala Cinema

10 Scala Cinema

MAP P2 ■ Siam Square, Soi 1 ■ 02 251 2861

Completed in 1967, the 900-seat Art Deco Scala harks back to the pre-multiplex period and has been well restored. The best place to catch a movie in Bangkok, it shows new releases in a classic setting, and offers fantastic value for money.

Cycleway over the river in the green surroundings of Bang Krajao

Children's Attractions

Roller coaster soaring over Dream World amusement park

1 Dream World

MAP T2 ▪ 62 Moo 1, Rangsit-Nakornnayok Road, Thanyaburi, Pathumthani ▪ 02 577 8666 ▪ Open 10am–5pm Mon–Fri, 10am–7pm Sat & Sun ▪ Adm ▪ www.dreamworld.co.th

Featuring a hanging roller coaster, a sightseeing train, water rides and various other amusements, the Dream World theme park comprises different areas, including Snow Town, Fairytale Land and Seven Wonders of the World.

2 Snake Farm

Founded as the Pasteur Institute in 1923, the Queen Saovabha Memorial Institute, better known as the Snake Farm, is now run by the Red Cross. Shows on snake handling and feeding are held every day (2:30pm Mon–Fri, 11am Sat & Sun), and venom-milking sessions of cobras and pit vipers take place on weekdays at 11am. Brave visitors can also get a souvenir photo with a snake around their neck *(see p85)*.

3 SEA LIFE Bangkok Ocean World

One of the largest aquariums in Southeast Asia, the superb SEA LIFE Bangkok Ocean World is divided into zones such as Ocean Tunnel and Rocky Shore. Attractions include the chance to dive with sharks. There are also a number of penguin and shark feeding sessions *(see p88)*.

SEA LIFE Bangkok Ocean World penguin

4 Kidzania

MAP P2 ▪ Floor 5, Siam Paragon, Rama I Road ▪ 02 683 1888 ▪ Open 10am–5pm Mon–Fri, 10:30am–8:30pm Sat, Sun & hols ▪ Adm ▪ www.kzbangkok.kidzania.com

Kids can play at being doctors and nurses, Japanese chefs, crime scene investigators, and even fortune tellers at this imaginative and varied activity centre in Bangkok.

5 Funarium

MAP T6 ▪ Soi 26, Sukhumvit Road, near Rama IV Road ▪ 02 665 6555 ▪ Open 9am–6pm Mon–Thu, 9am–7pm Fri–Sun ▪ Adm ▪ www.funarium.co.th

Children 13 years and under can partake in a number of activities at this huge indoor playground near the center of town. It has an arts and crafts room, cooking classes, a restaurant, and it hosts story telling and magic show events on weekends.

6 Bangkok Butterfly Garden and Insectarium

MAP T5 ▪ Suan Vachirabenchathat (Rotfai or Railway Park), Kamphaeng Phet 3 Road ▪ 02 272 4359 ▪ Open 8:30am–4:30pm Tue–Sun

Walking distance from Chatuchak Park subway station and Mo Chit Skytrain station, this park is home to over 500 butterflies. There is a study centre and a children's playground on site and one can rent bikes in the adjacent park, which has family-oriented cycle routes (see p63).

Beautifully shaded Lumphini Park

8 Children's Discovery Museum

MAP T5 ▪ Queen Sirikit Park, Kamphaengphet Road ▪ 02 272 4500 ▪ Open 10am–4pm Tue–Sun

Hands-on exhibits include a Science Discovery Zone, and Incredible Me, where children can learn about their bodies, senses, and emotions.

9 Lumphini Park

Named after the birthplace of the Buddha in Nepal, this is the only decent-sized park in the center of Bangkok. It has lots of shady trees and a large lake (see p86).

Exhibit at Bangkok Dolls Museum

7 Bangkok Dolls Museum

MAP T5 ▪ 85 Soi Mo Leng, Ratchaprarop Road ▪ 02 245 3008 ▪ Open 8am–5pm Tue–Sat ▪ www. bangkokdolls.com

This museum was created by Tongkorn Chandavimol in the 1950s after a visit to Japan, which aroused her interest in dolls from different countries and eras. The dolls here, from her own collection, are from all over the world. Handcrafted dolls can be bought in the adjacent workshop for B500.

10 Flow House

MAP T6 ▪ A-Square, Sukhumvit Soi 26 ▪ 02 108 5210 ▪ Open 2–10pm Mon–Fri, 10am–11pm Sat, Sun & hols ▪ Adm ▪ www.flowhousebangkok.com ▪ No children under 5

The wave-simulating surfing machine here is guaranteed to pacify the most restless of adolescents. There is a bit of a learning curve involved, so instructors are always on hand.

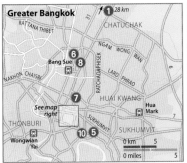

🔟 Bars and Clubs

Live music at Adhere the 13th

1 Adhere the 13th
MAP C2 ■ 13 Samsen Road ■ 08 9769 4613 ■ Open 6pm–midnight daily

This tiny hole-in-the-wall bar, popularly known as the Blues Bar, has a welcoming atmosphere, sociable pavement seats, and well-priced beer and cocktails. The Thai and expat bands play mostly blues and jazz, with special weekend events proving to be the big crowd-pullers.

2 Sky Bar
Famous for alfresco drinks, this standing-only bar featured in *The Hangover II*. It is built 902-ft (275-m) above the city's pavements, with almost 360-degree views. Come early to enjoy the stunning panoramas as the sun sets (see p92).

3 Saxophone
The music here is impressive with three sets every night, mixing jazz and acoustic with blues, rock, and reggae. Prices are moderate (see p93).

4 Ce La Vi
Bangkok's coolest nightclub pulls in a dress-to-impress crowd. Music varies by night from soulful beats, to hip-hop, to future house. There are booths, standing tables, a dance floor, and great views of the city from the 39th-floor Club Lounge (see p93).

5 Bamboo Bar
MAP M5 ■ Oriental Hotel, 48 Oriental Avenue ■ 02 659 9000 ■ Open 5pm–2am Fri & Sat, 5pm–1am Sun–Thu ■ www.mandarinoriental.com/bangkok

With its relaxed atmosphere and great lineups, this is a fantastic spot to unwind and listen to smooth jazz.

6 Maggie Choo's
Discreet and opulent, the prohibition era of 1930s Shanghai has been recreated in this trendy bar. Leather armchairs and couches are surrounded by Art Deco lamps and Khmer statues, and the brick walls are original – it was once a bank vault. There's live jazz later in the evenings and good food (see p93).

Shanghai prohibition-era decadence at Maggie Choo's

7 Levels

Each of the three party zones at this famous nightspot has its own atmosphere and vibe, from raucous house to sophisticated lounge music. Check out all three to experience the full effect (see p93).

8 Brown Sugar: The Jazz Boutique

MAP D3 ▪ 469 Wanchad Junction, Phra Sumen Road ▪ 02 282 0396 ▪ Open 11am–1am Tue–Thu & Sun, 11am–2am Fri–Sat ▪ www.brown sugarbangkok.com

The city's premier jazz venue is a restaurant and coffee house by day; at night it is a bar featuring an acoustic set followed by the resident jazz band.

Brown Sugar: The Jazz Boutique

9 Studio Lam

This small bar is run by the DJs of Zudrangma Records, who play *morlam*, folk music from northeastern Thailand, and an eclectic choice of beats from around the world on a massive, purpose-built sound system (see p100).

10 RCA

MAP T6 ▪ Rama IX Road, Soi 8

Royal City Avenue is a popular entertainment zone lined with trendy dance clubs, such as Route 66, as well as restaurants and noodle stands. Young city workers and students regard it as party central.

TOP 10 GAY BARS AND CLUBS

Gay bars in the Soi Twilight district

1 The Balcony
MAP P5 ▪ Silom Soi 4
At the heart of Bangkok's gay scene, the Balcony bar offers cheap food and great value evening happy hours.

2 The Stranger Bar
MAP P5 ▪ Silom Soi 4
This bar has three floors of dancing, daily cabaret shows, and a lounge area.

3 Disco Disco
MAP P5 ▪ Silom Soi 2
This bar-cum-disco is a one of the top places to see and be seen in Bangkok.

4 DJ Station
MAP P5 ▪ Silom Soi 2
A popular gay disco that is packed to the rafters almost every night.

5 The Expresso
MAP P5 ▪ Silom Soi 2
This bar is a good place to chill out and take in the action in Silom Soi.

6 X Boom
MAP P4 ▪ Surawong Road
The party only really gets going after midnight at this popular club.

7 G.O.D.
MAP P5 ▪ Silom Road (between Soi 2 and Soi 4)
Guys on Display is an aptly named gay bar that has a big dance area.

8 Telephone Pub
MAP P5 ▪ 114/11–13 Silom Soi 4
This pub is named for the phones that once offered table-to-table contact.

9 Fox and Cork
MAP P5 ▪ 104 Silom Soi 4
The good range of food served at this bar appeals to a classy crowd.

10 Dick's Café
MAP P5 ▪ Surawong Road
Elegant day-and-night café and bar with a Casablanca theme to the decor.

🔟 Restaurants

Lavish interior at Le Normandie, with calming river views

1 Le Normandie

An institution in the venerable Oriental Hotel, Le Normandie serves top-notch classic French food and has a relaxing ambience, lavish decor, views on the river, and impeccable service. Specialties include roast duck foie gras and Brittany half lobster, and the wine list offers over 200 French wines (see p91).

2 Bo.Lan

Thai food at its finest is served in this beautifully renovated wooden house. The menu is à la carte at lunchtime, and there are three set menus in the evening (including one vegetarian). All offer eclectic yet authentic Thai cuisine made from the finest organic ingredients (see p99).

Thai fine-dining at Bo.Lan

3 L'Atelier de Joël Robuchon

Considered the most important chef since Escoffier, Robuchon does French food that is elegant, rustic and imaginative. L'Atelier seats guests around an open kitchen. Thai cuisine influences some of the dishes. It's *très, très chic* (see p91).

4 Blue Elephant

Located in a European-style mansion, the Blue Elephant offers a menu of Royal Thai cuisine, ranging from classic staples to experimental creations. There are a number of tasty starters, and the salmon larb main is highly recommended. There's also a jazzy cocktail bar (see p99).

5 Issaya Siamese Club

Delicious Thai food with a contemporary twist is served in a 1920s mansion with private dining rooms. There's bright, furnishings and a garden outside. The chef's choices are indicated on the menu, including *yam hua plii* (banana flower salad with crunchy dressing) and *pla ob prik* (baked fish with a chili glaze (see p91).

6 Lenzi Tuscan Kitchen

Choosing the best Italian in Bangkok is hard, but Lenzi is a strong contender. The chef, formerly of the excellent Opus Wine Bar, has perfectly re-created the cuisine of his native Tuscany. The food and the service are excellent (see p91).

For a key to restaurant price ranges see p75

7 Eat Me

An art gallery and restaurant, Eat Me has changing exhibitions on the walls and alfresco seating on the covered balconies. The black truffle and Parmesan risotto and papardelle with rabbit *ragù* are among the many international specialties here. The desserts are excellent, too *(see p91)*.

8 Liu

A relative newcomer among Bangkok's Chinese restaurants, this place is becoming famous for its Peking duck. The *dong po* pork (stewed pork belly and black soy sauce served with Chinese buns), is also excellent. The atmosphere is quiet and elegant *(see p91)*.

9 Rong Mahal

Often named by Indians as the best Indian food in the city, Rong Mahal has been perfecting its fare for more than 20 years. There's live but discreet Indian music in the evenings. The views from its 26th-floor perch atop the Rembrandt Hotel are incredible *(see p91)*.

10 Gaggan

Consistently voted among the world's top 50 in *Restaurant* magazine, Gaggan makes progressive Indian food using molecular gastronomy techniques. With a relaxed ambience in a converted wooden house, it has panache in both menu and service *(see p91)*.

Relaxed dining area at Gaggan

TOP 10 CULINARY HIGHLIGHTS

Bowl of *tom yam kung*

1 Tom Yam Kung
Thailand's signature dish – a hot and spicy soup with chilies, lemongrass, and galangal – is typically served with prawns or seafood.

2 Phat Thai
Literally "Thai fry," this delicious noodle dish with beansprouts, peanuts, and eggs is a great lunchtime filler.

3 Kaeng Phanaeng
This thick curry made with coconut cream and spices is usually served with pork or chicken, plus a side of rice.

4 Nam Prik Num
This delicious, gooey dip made of pounded chilies and eggplant seems to typify Thai cuisine with its spicy taste and creamy texture.

5 Sticky Rice
Thais from the north and northeast of the country often press a ball of sticky rice into their dips and sauces.

6 Som Tam
Unripe (green) papaya is shredded finely and mixed with dried shrimp, lemon juice, tomatoes, peanuts, fish sauce, and chilies to make this salad.

7 Phat Pak Bung
Morning glory, one of Thailand's tastiest green vegetables, is fried with garlic and chilis in oyster sauce for this crunchy, nutritious dish.

8 Mango with Sticky Rice
A delicious dessert of ripe mango with sticky rice and a coconut milk sauce.

9 Coconut Custard
This dessert is a sweet concoction of coconut milk, eggs, and sugar.

10 Fruit Juices and Shakes
Most Thai fruits can be served as tasty, thirst-quenching juices, or shakes when mixed with yoghurt.

🔟 Markets and Shopping

Entrance to Asiatique the Riverfront

1 Asiatique the Riverfront
MAP S6 ■ Charoen Krung Road ■ Open 5pm–midnight daily ■ www.asiatique.com

This open-air night market and entertainment zone has hundreds of cool boutiques, restaurants, the cabaret show Calypso *(see p51)*, and a huge Ferris wheel. Despite being touristy, it's well done and good fun.

2 Siam Paragon
This mall connects directly with its two adjacent neighbours, Siam Center and Siam Discovery. While the featured items are mainly international luxury brands, there are also clothing and accessories from top Thai designers. All three offer a plethora of designer clothes, cosmetics, hairdressers, restaurants, cinemas, and book and music shops *(see p89)*.

Siam Paragon

3 Mahboonkrong
While most of Bangkok's shopping malls have a clinical, international feel to them, Mahboonkrong is totally Thai. Also known as MBK, this mall sprawls across six floors. It is packed with stalls selling souvenirs and cheap clothes. There are also bigger outlets selling jewelry and a branch of the Japanese Tokyu Department Store *(see p89)*.

4 Central World
MAP Q2 ■ Rama I Road ■ Open 10am–10pm daily

Bangkok's largest mall, accessible by Skywalk from Siam Paragon, has everything from designer items to funky boutiques, bookstores, and electronic equipment in more than 500 stores. There are also some excellent restaurants, 15 cinemas, a kids' zone, and an ice-skating rink within the complex.

5 Pratunam
Leaving Central World, a Skywalk leads to the Pratunam area, where things move downmarket a bit. Cluttering the sidewalk and spilling over into several small lanes, this bustling market is great for cheap clothes, as well as luggage, gadgets, souvenirs, and more. Platinum Fashion Mall nearby is a large air-conditioned version of Pratunam *(see p88)*.

6 Emporium and EmQuartier

MAP T6 ▪ Sukhumvit Road, near Soi 24 ▪ 02 269 1000 ▪ Open 10am–10pm daily ▪ www.emporium.co.th

These neighboring malls cover both sides of Sukhumvit Road, joined by a Skywalk. While the Emporium is dedicated to high fashion and some fine restaurants, the newer EmQuartier is more diverse and boutique-oriented. It also has a really lovely garden *(see p52)*.

7 Laai Sap Market

MAP P5 ▪ Silom Soi 5 ▪ Open 8am–5pm Mon–Fri

For a look at a real, authentic Bangkokian's street market – away from the more luxurious tourist equivalents – head to Laai Sap. There are small restaurants (busy with office workers at noon) and stalls selling inexpensive clothing and accessories. The market's name means "Money Melts," but it melts in small denominations here.

8 Terminal 21

MAP T6 ▪ Sukhumvit Road ▪ 02 108 0888 ▪ Open 10am–10pm daily ▪ www.terminal21.co.th

This huge mall resembles a futuristic airport terminal, and each of the nine floors is decorated in city themes, from San Francisco to Rome. Mid-range clothing and boutiques abound, as do good restaurants. The relaxed atmosphere here tends to attract a younger and more local clientele than many of the other Sukhumvit malls.

9 Pantip Plaza

MAP Q2 ▪ New Phetburi Road ▪ 02 250 1555 ▪ Open 10am–10pm daily ▪ www.pantipplaza.com

This IT mecca sells the latest computer programs and DVD movies, as well as digital cameras and other electronics. Although it is crammed with hardware and software, the mall is rife with counterfeit products. Despite regular police raids, vendors dealing in pirated goods stay in business thanks to their customers' huge appetite for such stuff.

Clothes at Sampeng Lane Market

10 Sampeng Lane Market

The market held on this narrow street is lined with shops selling household goods, fashion accessories, shoes, and clothing. Phahurat Road *(see p77)* leads into Sampeng Lane, and walking from one to the other feels like hopping from India to China *(see p78)*.

TOP 10 Bangkok for Free

1 Visit Temples

Most temples in Bangkok, such as Wat Mahathat and Wat Ratchabophit, are free to enter and offer a pleasant respite from the clamor of the city. All that is required is respectful dress and a quiet demeanor. Remove your shoes at the entrance of the largest building, sit for a while, and absorb the calming atmosphere.

Wat Ratchabophit's entrance

2 Thai Boxing at MBK Shopping Center

MAP P3 ■ Corner of Phaya Thai and Rama I Roads ■ 02 620 9000 ■ Bouts 6pm Wednesday

Authentic *muay Thai* matches are held outside Tokyu Department Store and run into the evening. These are not the watered-down exhibition matches held at tourist venues – the crowd is raucous and the punches and kicks are real *(see p49)*.

3 Puppet Show at Artist's House in Khlong Bang Luang

MAP S6 ■ Soi Wat Thong Sala Ngarm, Thonburi ■ (083) 034 9858 ■ Performances 2pm daily

On the Thonburi side of the river, this place is a bit hard to find but worth the effort. A project by a local artist here keeps Thai culture alive with traditional Thai puppet shows. There are also free art exhibits and, on weekends, a floating market.

4 Phra Athit Park Aerobics

MAP C2 ■ Phra Athit Road

Next to the Prom Phra Sumen Fort, on the Chao Phraya River, this small but beautiful park hosts informal aerobics classes starting an hour before sunset every day. A leader on stage shows the movements and gives encouragement to all the exercisers taking part.

5 Bangkok Art & Culture Centre

MAP P2 ■ Corner of Phaya Thai and Rama I Roads ■ 02 214 6630 ■ www.bacc.or.th

An oasis of calm amid the malls in Bangkok's prime shopping zone, the BACC is a striking, white contemporary art museum that always has a wide choice of exhibitions and events on.

6 Thai Dancing at Erawan Shrine

This holy shrine in Bangkok's shopping district venerates the Hindu God Brahma. Thais come to make offerings of flowers and incense and to commission the resident Thai classical dancers to perform for the spirits *(see p86)*.

Thai dancers at Erawan Shrine

T'ai chi practitioners in Lumphini Park

⑦ Lumphini Park T'ai Chi

As soon as dawn breaks, aficionados of this ancient Chinese dance-like practice start their routines. Visitors are always very welcome to paricipate: simply stand at the back of the group and follow the movements (see p86).

⑧ Bangkok Butterfly Garden

A respite from the nearby weekend market, this park within a park has open areas where the butterflies live, as well as displays of various specimens under glass (see p55).

Bangkok Butterfly Garden

⑨ Neilson Hays Library Art Galleries

MAP N5 ■ 195 Surawong Road ■ 02 233 1731 ■ Open 9:30am–5pm Tues–Sun ■ www.neilsonhayslibrary.com

Housed in a beautiful Neo-Classical building, the private Neilson Hays Library has two excellent art galleries: the Rotunda and the Garden Café.

⑩ Meditation Course at Wat Mahathat

Introductory walk-in courses in Buddhist meditation start at 7am, 1pm, and 6pm and cover both seated and walking techniques. A brief lecture introduces the three-hour session. The temple also offers longer residential courses, with food and accommodation provided; a donation is usually expected for these courses (see p44).

TOP 10 MONEY-SAVING TIPS

1 Get a local SIM card for your phone or tablet. Kiosks offer short-term plans at the airport and in all city malls. Data speeds are very good in Bangkok.

2 All shopping malls have air-conditioned food courts, often in the basement, where a variety of vendors offer local specialties for much less than you would pay in restaurants.

3 Bangkok's mass transit systems – the MRT, BTS Skytrain, and Airport Rail Link – cover most of the city.

4 The Chao Phraya Express Boat Service is a great way to see all the river sights and beat the traffic.

5 *Bangkok 101* and *The Big Chilli* are great magazines that give a current picture of free events, discounts, and promotions in the city. *BK* magazine is free but less interesting.

6 Bangkok's new hostels are clean and cheap. Try Suk 11 (see p117).

7 Bargaining is perfectly appropriate for any non-food item in a street market. Offer 50 percent and keep on smiling.

8 Imported alcoholic drinks are taxed up to 300 percent here, but the local beers (such as Singha, Leo, and Chang) are good, as is the rum – try Sang Som with soda and a squeeze of lime.

9 Traditional massage venues do not offer the luxury that you will find in the spas, but these ubiquitous shops offer good body or foot massages at very reasonable prices.

10 If you make any significant purchases, you can get a refund of the 7 percent VAT when leaving Thailand.

Food court of Siam Paragon

🔟 Festivals

1 Visaka Puja
Citywide ▪ May

The holiest day of the Buddhist calendar commemorates the Buddha's birth, enlightenment, and death. Occurring on the day of the full-moon, the evening candlelit procession around the temple is notable, especially at Wat Benjamabophit *(p44)*.

Revellers seeing in Chinese New Year

2 Chinese New Year
Chinatown ▪ Jan or Feb

This week-long Thai-Chinese celebration has lion dances in the street, lots of loud firecrackers, and colorful activities in temples.

3 Makha Puja
Citywide ▪ Feb or Mar

This annual Buddhist festival, held at the full moon, celebrates the Buddha's first sermon to 1,250 disciples, starting the dissemination of the *dhamma*.

Monks observing Makha Puja at Wat Phra Dhammakaya

4 Songkran
Citywide ▪ Mid–Apr

Thai New Year is the country's most chaotic and raucous festival. People throw water over each other as a symbolic form of cleansing to usher in the new year, and passers-by are not spared. Perhaps for its novelty value, this festival is particularly popular among foreign visitors.

5 Royal Ploughing Ceremony
Sanam Luang ▪ Early May

This annual event is designed to give an auspicious start to the new planting season. Sacred white oxen are used to plough a ritual field in Sanam Luang *(see p69)* near the Grand Palace *(see pp12–13)*, which is then sown with rice seeds blessed by the king. Farmers rush to collect the seeds to plant in their own fields.

6 International Festival of Dance and Music
Thailand Cultural Centre ▪ Sep & Oct

Since 1999, Bangkok's premier international arts festival has been held at the Thailand Cultural Centre *(see p50)* in September and October each year. It features acts from around the world, along with some of Thailand's best performers. The focus of the festival is mainly on opera, ballet, and classical music, though jazz and modern dance are represented as well.

7 Loy Krathong
Citywide ■ Nov

This festival, usually held in November, offers homage to the goddess of the waters for providing a successful harvest. Beautiful *krathong* (small decorated floats) are released onto the river at night while fireworks light up the sky.

8 Wat Saket Fair
Golden Mount ■ Nov

Temple fairs in Thailand are like village fêtes in the West, and this one at Wat Saket and the Golden Mount (see p70), held just before or after Loy Krathong, is a good example. It has a great atmosphere, with music, theater and lots of kids having fun.

Performers at Wat Saket fair

9 Bangkok World Film Festival
www.worldfilmbkk.com ■ Jan

Held each year, usually in January, this film festival showcases over 100 films from all around the world, with a particular emphasis on emerging film-makers throughout Asia.

10 King Bhumibol's Birthday
Citywide ■ Dec

Celebrated on December 5, this is both a national holiday and Fathers' Day, Thais have long celebrated the birthday of Rama IX, who died in late 2016. It's possible that this will remain on the calendar, with the new king Vajiralongkorn's birthday on July 28 added as a further holiday.

TOP 10 UP-COUNTRY FESTIVALS

Spirit costumes at Phi Ta Khon

1 Chiang Mai Flower Festival
First weekend, Feb
A parade of marching bands precedes floats bedecked with flowers.

2 ASEAN Barred Ground Dove Festival
First week, Mar
This dove-singing contest attracts competitors from far and wide to Yala.

3 Pattaya Music Festival
Mar
Thai musicians and international acts play in a wide variety of styles.

4 Poy Sang Long
First weekend, Apr
A Shan festival held in Chiang Mai and Mae Hong Son in which ordaining novices are paraded round the streets.

5 Rocket Festival
May
In the northeast, especially Yasothon, home-made rockets are fired to trigger the start of the monsoons.

6 Hua Hin Jazz Festival
Jun
This beach festival attracts big names.

7 Phi Ta Khon
Jun/Jul
Locals in Dan Sai dress as spirits for this wild and colorful event in Loei province.

8 Phuket Vegetarian Festival
Oct
Bizarre acts of self-mortification draw in the crowds for nine days.

9 Lanna Boat Races
Oct/Nov
At the end of the Buddhist Lent; the most exciting are in Nan Province.

10 Elephant Round-Up
Nov
Surin, in the northeast, is the venue for this pachyderm extravaganza.

Bangkok
Area by Area

The modern, glittering skyline
of Bangkok after dark

TOP 10 Old City

Bangkok's historical and spiritual heart lies in the Old City. When Chao Phraya Chakri, later pronounced Rama I, assumed the throne in 1782, he had a canal dug across a neck of land on the east bank of the Chao Phraya River to create an island that emulated the former capital at Ayutthaya. This island became known as Rattanakosin; now, it and the area to its east are known as the Old City. Here stand the Grand Palace, once home of the royal family, and Wat Phra Kaeo, a glittering temple that houses the Emerald Buddha, as well as several important temples, museums, universities, and Sanam Luang.

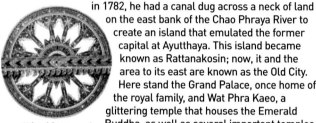

Wheel from royal funeral chariot

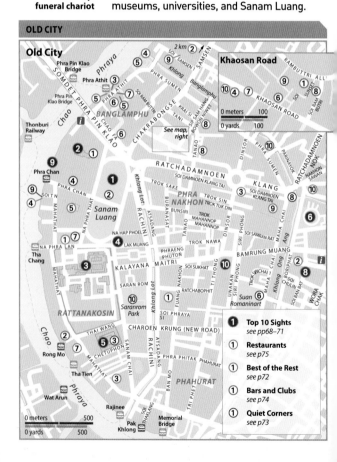

OLD CITY

Old City

Khaosan Road

1 Top 10 Sights
see pp68–71

1 Restaurants
see p75

1 Best of the Rest
see p72

1 Bars and Clubs
see p74

1 Quiet Corners
see p73

1 Sanam Luang
MAP B3 ▪ Na Phra Lan Road

Considering Bangkok's congested streets and high-rise buildings, it is amazing that a large open area such as Sanam Luang, or Royal Field, could exist at all. Its importance for certain royal ceremonies, such as cremation rites of royalty, guarantee that this precious patch of land will never be developed into offices or malls. From February to April, people fly kites here, and fortune tellers ply their trade.

2 National Museum
Located near the northern end of Rattanakosin Island, the National Museum (see pp16–17) is the repository of significant Thai art. Its huge size reflects the depth of Thai artistic achievement. Exhibits range from Dvaravati sculptures over 1,000 years old, to lavish funeral chariots, and the delightful Buddhaisawan Chapel, which houses the Phra Sihing Buddha image, considered second in importance only to the Emerald Buddha in Wat Phra Kaeo.

3 Grand Palace and Wat Phra Kaeo
In the center of Rattanakosin Island, the huge complex that contains the Grand Palace and Wat Phra Kaeo is one of Asia's unforgettable sights. It is the best place for an introduction to Thai architecture and art. While the palace is strongly influenced by Italian Renaissance architecture, the temple complex is totally Thai, from the towering *bot* (ordination hall) that holds the Emerald Buddha to the slender lines of the Phra Si Rattana Chedi and the *Ramakien* murals that decorate the galleries on all sides (see pp12–15).

Grand Palace and Wat Phra Kaeo

4 Lak Muang
MAP C4 ▪ Corner of Ratchadamnoen and Lak Muang roads ▪ Open 8:30am–5:30pm daily

This shrine houses the city pillar of Bangkok, erected by Rama I in 1782 and believed to contain the city's guardian spirit, Jao Pho Lak Muang. Also in the shrine is the city pillar of Thonburi, now part of Greater Bangkok. Both pillars are made of wood with lotus-shaped crowns and are painted gold. Lak Muang is always busy with devotees.

City pillars at Lak Muang

5 Wat Pho
Officially Wat Phra Chetuphon, this is Bangkok's oldest and largest temple and a welcoming center of learning, particularly of the massage techniques for which it is famous. While Wat Phra Kaeo impresses with bejeweled monuments, Wat Pho's charms are more subtle. The main attraction is the 150-ft (46-m) long Reclining Buddha that fills a *wihan* (assembly hall) in the compound's northwest corner, but it can be just as much fun exploring quieter corners of the grounds and chatting with the monks, schoolchildren, and massage practitioners (see pp18–19).

6 Wat Saket and the Golden Mount

MAP E3 (Wat Saket) and D3 (Golden Mount) ▪ 344 Chakkaphatdi Phong ▪ 02 621 2280 ▪ Open 8am–5pm daily ▪ Adm (for Golden Mount)

This was one of the first temples built when the city was founded in the late 1700s, initially as a crematorium for the common people. Fine murals adorn the walls of the *wihan* (assembly hall). Climb the 320 steps to the summit of the Golden Mount, a 250-ft (76-m) high artificial hill surmounted by a graceful golden, bell-shaped *chedi* (stupa), for fine views of the Old City skyline.

Monk making bowls at Soi Ban Baat

SPIRITS IN THAI SOCIETY

Lak Muang, the Amulet Market, and spirit houses (shrines dedicated to the spirit of the land on which a house is built) are all animist manifestations, which demonstrate that Thai religious belief is not limited to Buddhism. In fact, Buddhism's success here is partly due to its assimilation of aspects of other belief systems, such as Hinduism.

7 River and Canal Tour

Many visitors to Bangkok want to take a trip on the river and nearby canals to get a sense of how the city was before the motor car and catch a glimpse of traditional canal-side life. There are many tours that may be organized via your hotel or guesthouse. Alternatively, negotiate a price with a longtail-boat owner at any of the principal piers, and arrange a customized tour *(see pp20–21)*.

8 Soi Ban Baat

MAP D4 ▪ Soi Ban Baat, Boriphat Road

Buddhist monks have few material possessions – the *baat* (alms bowl) is one of them. Early each morning the bowls are filled with food offerings by devout Buddhists. They are mostly made in factories, but in Soi Ban Baat, or Monk's Bowl Village, there are still a few families that beat out the bowls by hand. Traditionally, these *baat* are made of eight strips of metal to represent the Eightfold Path of Buddhism. First, they are welded in a kiln, then shaped and filed smooth, and finally fired again.

9 Amulet Market

MAP B4 ▪ Mahathat Road and small lanes ▪ Open 8am–6pm daily

There is a strong belief among Thais that small images of the Buddha,

Boating down a canal

famous kings, or even tigers' teeth worn as pendants can provide protection from misfortune. It is, therefore, quite common to see people wearing a string of such amulets around the neck, and some even become ardent collectors of amulets. One of the best places to see this faith demonstrated is in the Amulet Market on the streets around Wat Mahathat, where potential buyers will carefully scrutinize the tiny objects with magnifying glasses and quiz the vendor to ascertain the amulet's properties.

Traditional art at Wat Suthat

⑩ Wat Suthat

MAP D4 ▪ 146 Bamrung Muang Road ▪ 02 224 9845 ▪ Open 8:30am–9pm daily ▪ Adm

Begun in 1807 by Rama I (r.1782–1807) and completed by his successors, Wat Suthat is one of Bangkok's most important temples. Fronted by the towering Sao Ching Cha, a giant swing that was once used for a Brahmin ceremony, the compound has the tallest *wihan* in the city, especially constructed to accommodate the Phra Sri Sakyamuni Buddha, a 26-ft (8-m) tall 14th-century Sukhothai image. The murals in the *wihan* are beautifully detailed, and the temple grounds include four lovely bronze horses.

A STROLL THROUGH THE OLD CITY

▶ MORNING

Begin your exploration of the Old City at **Wat Saket**, where you can climb the **Golden Mount** to enjoy a wonderful, panoramic view of the area. From here walk south along Boriphat Road until you reach **Soi Ban Baat**, where alms bowls are beaten out of strips of metal. Go back up Boriphat Road, then left into **Bamrung Muang Road** (*see p72*) where shops sell Buddha images and temple paraphernalia. When you reach the unmissable **Sao Ching Cha**, turn into **Wat Suthat** and appreciate the superb carvings and paintings on display. Continue over the Klong and turn right onto **Sanam Chai** for the lush green lawns of **Sanam Luang** (*see p69*). For lunch, follow the road at the southern end of the park to a row of charming 19th-century shops and the **Krisa Coffee Shop** (*see p75*), serving tasty Thai dishes.

AFTERNOON

After lunch, head east again, between Sanam Luang and the walls around **Wat Phra Kaeo** (*see pp12–15*). Straight ahead stands the **Lak Muang** (*see p69*) shrine where you can watch supplicants making offerings and praying. Wander west again between **Sanam Luang** and Wat Phra Kaeo (*see p69*), to admire paintings at the **Silpakorn University Art Exhibition Hall** (*see p73*). Buy a lucky charm at the fascinating **Amulet Market** or in the small lanes off it. Have a cool drink at **S&P Restaurant** (*see p75*) at the riverside pier to round off your day's wander in the Old City.

See map on p68 ➤

The Best of the Rest

1 Wat Ratchabophit

The design of this temple is based on the circular *chedi* (stupa) at Nakhon Pathom. The highlights include inlay work on the doors and windows of the *bot* (ordination hall), and colorful tiles in the cloisters (see p45).

Inlay work at Wat Ratchabophit

2 Bamrung Muang Road

MAP D4

Originally an elephant trail, this was one of the first roads to be paved in Bangkok. Its shops sell temple necessities such as monks' robes, candles, incense, and Buddha images.

3 Museum of Siam

MAP C5 ■ Sanam Chai Road ■ 02 225 2777 ■ Open 10am–6pm Tue–Sun ■ Adm ■ www.museum siam.org

Spread over three floors, this museum has fascinating interactive exhibits that explore Thai history and culture, Buddhism, and more.

4 Phra Sumen Fort

MAP C2 ■ Phra Athit Road

This octagonal brick-and-stucco fort, one of 14 watchtowers, was built in 1783 to defend the city from attack.

Phra Sumen Fort

5 Wat Mahathat

This royal temple today serves as the headquarters of Mahachulalongkorn Buddhist University and is home to the respected Vipassana Meditation Center (see p44).

6 National Gallery

MAP C3 ■ 4 Chao Fa Road ■ 02 281 2224 ■ Open 9am–4pm Wed–Sun ■ Adm

Located in a building that once housed the Royal Mint, this is Bangkok's principal art gallery. It features the work of established and emerging Thai artists.

7 Khao San Road

MAP C3

Besides several budget guesthouses, this bustling backpacker's ghetto has a variety of souvenir shops, market stalls, and restaurants.

8 Wat Bowoniwet

MAP C2 ■ 240 Phra Sumen Road ■ 02 280 0869 ■ Open 8am–5pm daily ■ www.watbowon.org

The base of the Tammayut sect of Buddhism, this temple has some striking murals (see p44).

9 Loha Prasat and Wat Ratchanadda

MAP D3 ■ 2 Maha Chai Road ■ 02 224 8807 ■ Open 9am–5pm daily

The Loha Prasat (or "iron castle") is a stepped, seven-tiered pyramid with 37 metal spires. Its grounds are shared with Wat Ratchanadda.

10 King Prajadhipok (Rama VII) Museum

MAP D3 ■ 2 Lan Luang Road ■ 02 280 3413 ■ Open 9am–4pm Tue–Sun ■ Adm

This state-of-the-art museum looks at the events of 1925–35, which included the transition of Siam from absolute to constitutional monarchy.

Quiet Corners

1 Buddhaisawan Chapel, National Museum

After learning about Thai history in the National Museum, settle down on the cool teak floorboards of this chapel to meditate, in front of the Phra Sihing Buddha image *(see p16)*.

Artwork, Buddhaisawan Chapel

2 Sanam Luang

This open grassy area has several benches in the shade of trees that offer rest to weary legs *(see p69)*.

3 Massage Pavilion, Wat Pho

Traditional Thai massage is a great help for aching legs and a muddled mind. Come here for some of the country's best masseurs *(see p18)*.

4 Thammasat University

MAP B3 ▪ Maharat Road

Thailand's second-oldest university, opened in 1934, lies just upstream from the Amulet Market. There are some nice spots for resting, and a food court catering to the students.

5 Santichaiprakhan Park

MAP C2 ▪ Phra Athit Road ▪ Open 5am–10pm daily

Looking out over the Chao Phraya River, this park makes an excellent place to sit and see the world go by. Visitors can also join the aerobics class held here at dusk every day.

6 Corrections Museum, Romaninart Park

MAP D4 ▪ Maha Chai Road ▪ 02 226 1704 ▪ Open 5am–9pm daily

Formerly the site of a prison, this park now has ponds, fountains, shaded paths, and a museum which displays instruments of punishment.

7 Silpakorn University Art Exhibition Hall

MAP B4 ▪ Na Phra Lan Road ▪ 02 221 3841 ▪ Open 9am–7pm Mon–Fri, 9am–4pm Sat

Set inside the country's leading art school, this tranquil gallery features works by teachers, students, and artists-in-residence at the university.

8 Mahakan Fort

MAP D3 ▪ Maha Chan and Ratchadamnoen roads

This octagonal fort is one of two surviving watchtowers of the 14 that ringed the city. The park beside it is a great place to stop and relax.

9 Riverside Restaurants, Tha Maharat

MAP B3 ▪ Mahathat Road

The cool river breeze makes this complex of restaurants one of the best places to recover from a tiring walk.

Walking in tranquil Saranrom Park

10 Saranrom Park

MAP C4 ▪ Rachini Road ▪ Open 5am–9pm daily

With shady trees, fountains, and benches, this park is a great place to take a break after trekking round the Grand Palace or Wat Pho.

See map on p68

Bars and Clubs

Pre-party drinks at Molly 31

1 Molly 31
MAP C3 ■ 146 Rambuttri Road
■ Open 4pm–3am daily

In a colonial-style building, this classy bar and club has a live band on the ground floor and a DJ upstairs.

2 Boh
MAP B5 ■ 230 Tha Tien ■ 02 622 3081 ■ Open 5pm–1am daily

This bar has an excellent view across the Chao Phraya River to Wat Arun, making it great for a sundowner.

3 Sheepshank
MAP B2 ■ Phra Athit express-boat pier ■ 02 629 5165 ■ Open 5pm–1am Tue–Sun

Cool industrial-looking gastropub set in an old boat repair yard by the river. It serves American and Japanese craft beers.

4 Hippie de Bar
MAP C3 ■ 46 Khao San Road ■ 02 629 3508 ■ Open 4pm–2am daily

A fashionable courtyard bar and boutique with a retro look, Hippie de Bar attracts a diverse crowd.

5 Jazz Happens
MAP B2 ■ Phra Athit Road ■ 02 282 9934 ■ Open 7pm–1am Fri–Wed

There's live jazz every night at this cozy grassroots bar with sociable pavement tables.

6 The Club
MAP C3 ■ 123 Khao San Rd ■ 02 629 2255 ■ Open 9pm–3am daily

A lively atmosphere, vast dance floor, and music from techno to trance pull in the crowds here.

7 Dickinson's Culture Cafe
MAP C2 ■ 64 Phra Athit Road ■ (089) 497 8422 ■ Open noon–2am Mon–Fri, 5pm–2am Sat & Sun

Music starts here at about 9pm, with techno, underground house, and trance.

8 999 West
MAP C2 ■ 108/5-6 Rambuttri Road ■ 02 629 2474 ■ Open 5pm–2am daily

This Wild West saloon-style bar, with DJs and live bands, lies in the heart of the Khao San backpacker area.

9 Roof Bar
MAP C3 ■ 3rd floor, Centre Point Plaza, Khao San Road ■ 02 629 2300 ■ Open 4:30pm–1:30am daily

Watch live bands with an amazing view from the balcony. It's a great spot to enjoy fresh air and good fun.

10 Brown Sugar: The Jazz Boutique

This long-established jazz bar, one of Bangkok's truly iconic night-time venues, attracts some exceptionally talented musicians. There is live music every night *(see p56)*.

Brown Sugar: The Jazz Boutique

Restaurants

PRICE CATEGORIES

For a meal for one with one or two dishes and a soft drink, including service.

B under B200   BB B200–1,000
BBB over B1,000

1 Krisa Coffee Shop
MAP B4 ▪ Na Phra Lan Road
▪ 02 225 2680 ▪ Open 9:30am–5pm
Mon–Sat ▪ B

Krisa is an ideal place to stop for a light Thai lunch and a refreshing cold drink before or after a visit to the Grand Palace.

2 Kaloang Home Kitchen
MAP D1 ▪ 2 Soi Wat
Tevarakunchorn ▪ 02 281 9228
▪ Open 11am–10pm daily ▪ BB

Hidden behind the National Library, this simple, alfresco riverside venue offers guests an excellent menu of inexpensive Thai cuisine.

3 Methavalai Sorn Daeng
MAP D3 ▪ 78/2 Ratchad-
amnoen Khlang Road ▪ 02 224 3088
▪ Open 10:30am–11pm daily ▪ BB

Open since 1957, this place is popular with locals of a certain age, since it recalls Bangkok before it became Westernized. Expect starched white tablecloths and high-class Thai cuisine.

4 S&P, Maharat Pier
MAP B3 ▪ Maharat Pier ▪ Open
10am–10pm daily ▪ B

Part of a countrywide chain of restaurants, S&P turns out tasty Thai food, ice creams, and cakes. A breezy riverside terrace is part of the appeal at this branch.

5 Aquatini
MAP B2 ▪ Navalai River Resort,
45 Phra Athit Road (seep 116) ▪ 02
280 9955 ▪ Open 6:30am–midnight
daily ▪ www.navalai.com ▪ BB

On a breezy riverfront deck, this hotel restaurant serves reasonably priced Thai food, especially seafood.

6 Hemlock
MAP B2 ▪ 56 Phra Athit Road
▪ 02 282 7507 ▪ Open 5–11pm Mon–
Sat ▪ BB

A small, trendy café, Hemlock offers many unusual dishes, including several vegetarian options.

7 Rub Aroon
MAP B5 ▪ Maharat Road
▪ 02 622 2312 ▪ Open 10am–6:30pm
daily ▪ B

This small shophouse has both inside and outside seating, a varied menu of staple Thai dishes, and plenty of refreshing drinks.

Relaxing at May Kaidee

8 May Kaidee
MAP C3 ▪ 59 Tanao Road
▪ 02 629 4413 ▪ Open 9am–10pm
daily ▪ www.maykaidee.com ▪ B

This restaurant serves delicious and cheap vegetarian, vegan, and cold food dishes. It also has its own cookery school.

9 Somsong Pochana
MAP C2 ▪ Soi 1, Samsen
Road ▪ Open 9am–4pm daily ▪ B

Traditional Sukhothai-style noodles are served to diners at this excellent little lunch spot.

10 Tom Yam Kung
MAP C3 ▪ Khao San Rd
▪ 02 629 1818 ▪ Open 11am–1am
daily ▪ BB

Named for Thailand's signature dish, a sour and spicy shrimp soup, Tom Yam Kung has an extensive menu.

See map on p68

TOP 10 Chinatown

At the time of Bangkok's founding in 1782 *(see p40)*, Chinese immigrants were moved out of Rattanakosin Island to make way for the Grand Palace and government buildings. They settled to the south of Rattanakosin Island beside the Chao Phraya River. These days Chinatown is one of the most colorful and congested areas of the city, and though it lacks the grand monuments of the Old City, it is fascinating for its maze of alleys, markets, gaudy temples, and gold shops. Sharing this crowded part of the capital with the Chinese is a small community of Indians in a sub-district known as Little India, with the cloth market of Phahurat at its heart.

Golden Buddha, Wat Traimit

① Golden Buddha, Wat Traimit

MAP F6 ▪ 661 Charoen Krung Road
▪ 02 225 9775 ▪ Open 8am–5pm daily
▪ Adm

There are thousands of gold-leaf smothered Buddha images in Thailand, but the Golden Buddha is made of solid gold – all 12,000 lb (5,500 kg) of it. This fact was revealed only in 1955 when it was accidentally dropped, exposing its gold interior. The 13-ft (4-m) tall, 13th-century Sukhothai Buddha is housed in a glittering, three-story shrine.

CHINATOWN

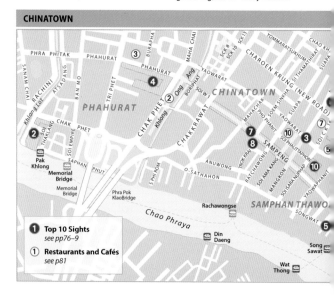

① **Top 10 Sights**
see pp76–9

① **Restaurants and Cafés**
see p81

2 Pak Khlong Market

MAP C5 ■ Chakphet Road ■ Open 24 hours daily

The sights, sounds, and smells at Bangkok's biggest flower, fruit, and vegetable market threaten to cause sensory overload. Throughout the night, boats laden with jasmine, lotus, and carnations unload their cargo, and at dawn the colorful displays of blooms and tropical fruits are at their best. The market is at its busiest in the mornings.

Gold shops along Yaowarat Road

3 Yaowarat Road

MAP E5 ■ Shops open 8am–10pm daily

The heart of Chinatown's gold trade, this one-way street boasts over 100 gold shops. Painted bright red, these shops flaunt glittering displays of necklaces and bracelets. The high volume of vehicles here often makes traffic come to a complete halt, and each evening the street gets even busier as foodstalls and vendors occupy every inch of space available.

4 Phahurat Market (Little India)

MAP C5 ■ Phahurat Road ■ Open 9am–6pm daily

Crossing the road in Bangkok's Chinatown can seem like traveling from China to India in the blink of an eye. An enclave within an enclave, Little India, mostly concentrated along Phahurat Road and the block to the south, shows that Indians and Chinese share a love of commerce. Saris and rainbow-colored bolts of cloth are stacked to the rooftops of the cramped shophouses and spill onto the streets. Tiny teahouses and shops selling offerings for Hindu temples complete the scene.

5 Songwat Road

MAP E6

Songwat Road runs parallel to the Chao Phraya River, and though the riverside piers and wharves are less busy now than a century ago, many companies still have their warehouses in this area, especially those in the rice trade. A stroll along this road and the small lanes that lead down to the river conjures up something of the atmosphere of Chinatown in bygone days. At its western end, Songwat Road leads to Pak Khlong, the flower market.

Wat Mangkon Kamalawat, Chinatown's most revered temple

⑥ Wat Mangkon Kamalawat (Wat Leng Noi Yee)

MAP E5 ▪ Charoen Krung Road ▪ 02 222 3975 ▪ Open 6am–6pm daily

Established in 1871, this is the most important of Chinatown's many Chinese temples. Wat Mangkon Kamalawat, or Dragon Flower Temple, is particularly active during the Vegetarian Festival in October, when devotees flock here to make offerings. Also known as Wat Leng Noi Yee, it has an impressive entrance gateway and the complex contains Buddhist, Taoist, and Confucian shrines. It is constantly busy with people making offerings, and vendors selling religious goods outside the temple do a brisk business.

YAOWARAT GOLD

The strong Chinese influence on Thai culture is evident in the love many Thais have for gold, a traditionally Chinese commodity. Thais display their status by wearing chunky bracelets and thick-linked watch straps. Gold in Bangkok is sold not by ounce but by baht, and some see it as more reliable than the country's currency.

⑦ Sampeng Lane

MAP L3 ▪ Open 8am–8pm daily

This narrow, frenetic lane, also known as Soi Wanit 1, stretches for about half a mile (1 km) through the very heart of Chinatown and is not for the fainthearted. Cars cannot even squeeze their way down here, but motorbikes and porters carrying stacks of goods try to weave through the slow-moving sea of humanity. People pause every few steps to examine the goods on offer – from computer games, to toys and clothes.

⑧ Wat Ga Buang Kim

MAP D6 ▪ Trok Krai, Anuwong Road

Set around a small, enclosed courtyard, this neighborhood temple is remarkable for its beautifully ornamented "vegetarian hall," which has an altar framed by intricately carved, gold-painted miniatures. The hall's outer wall is decorated with tableaux as well, and finely crafted ceramic figurines drawn from Chinese opera stories adorn the doorway at the top of the stairs. A second building in the temple compound functions as a stage for Chinese opera performances.

⑨ Talad Kao and Talad Mai

MAP E6 ▪ Soi Isara Nuphap
▪ Talad Kao: open 4–11am daily;
Talad Mai: open 4am–6pm daily

These two fresh-produce markets are piled high with fish, mushrooms, mangoes, curry pastes, Chinese herbs, and spices. The Talad Kao, or Old Market, has been open for trade since the late 18th century, while the Talad Mai, or New Market, is about 100 years old. Together, they have earned themselves a good name for high-quality meat, fish, vegetables, and fruits. They remain particularly busy during the Chinese New Year. The old market is frantic at dawn, but winds down before lunchtime, while the new one continues to operate until evening.

⑩ Hua Lampong Station

MAP F6 ▪ Rama IV Road ▪
02 225 6964

Initiated by Rama V (see p40), Hua Lampong Station was built just before World War I by Dutch archi-tects. Despite several revamps since then, the basic shell remains unchanged, making this train station one of Bangkok's most easily recognizable landmarks. This is the place where many out-of-towners begin their big city experience as they arrive at the railroad terminal and are more often than not preoccupied with avoiding scams rather than admiring the station's vaulted roof or mural paintings.

Monks at Hua Lampong Station

EXPLORING CHINATOWN AND LITTLE INDIA

Phra Phitak Road · Phaharat Road · Soi Isara Nuphap · Yaowarat Road · Charoen Krung Road · Little India · Royal India · Tha Rachini · Pak Khlong Market · Sampeng Lane · Wat Traimit, Golden Buddha

▶ MORNING

Traffic can be a nightmare at any time in Chinatown, so take the public ferry to Tha Rachini, at around 9am. Take the first right on leaving the pier, cross the canal and go right again into **Pak Khlong Market** (see p77), which should be at its busiest and best at this time. Next, head north up Atsadang Road and then turn right into Phra Phitak Road. Within a couple of short blocks this becomes Phahurat Road, and you are transported to **Little India** (see p77). Keep walking straight through until you reach Chak Phet Road. Have a delicious north Indian lunch at the **Royal India** (see p81) restaurant.

AFTERNOON

With your batteries recharged, plunge into **Sampeng Lane** with its kitsch gadgets and wind-up toys. Make sure that your wallet or purse is well hidden as this is a pickpocket's paradise. When you reach Soi Isara Nuphap, turn left and wander past all the Chinese herbalists and phar-macists on your way to **Yaowarat Road** (see p77). Turn right here and notice the profusion of gold shops, all painted bright red with vibrant gold lettering, and most with an armed guard on duty. Where Yaowarat Road meets Charoen Krung Road, cross to the east side of the street and enter the temple of **Wat Traimit** (see p76). Sit down for a few moments to rest and admire the superb craftsmanship of the **Golden Buddha** (see p76) and enjoy a tranquil end to the day.

See map on pp76–7

What to Buy

1 Flowers
Pak Khlong Market (see p77) is the place to buy fresh flowers – either individual cut blooms or a bouquet mixing a few favorites. Temperate flowers such as roses mingle with orchids and lotus ginger.

2 Gold
If you are seeking some gold ornamenta- tion, check out the gold shops along Yaowarat Road (see p78), which sell 23-carat gold in a wide variety of designs.

Lotus buds

3 Textiles
The fantastic range of textiles on sale in Chinatown, and particu- larly in Phahurat Market (see p77), is enough to tempt many visitors to take home a bolt of cloth or some inexpensive ready-made garments.

Shop staff preparing packets of tea

4 Tea
Green tea and black tea, loose or packaged, is sold throughout Chinatown, and is consumed in great quantities by the Chinese themselves. Fresh markets and herbalists would be the best places for you to sniff out a good brew.

5 Incense
For the Chinese, incense is essential, particularly for making offerings, and several shops in Chinatown sell incense in coils, pyramids, small sticks, and big sticks that burn for hours.

6 Fashion Accessories
There is nothing exclusive about the cheap trinkets on sale throughout Chinatown, particularly along Sampeng Lane (see p79). Plastic earrings, strings of beads, cuddly mobile phone covers, and sequined handbags are just a few of the items on offer.

7 Ceramics
Most of the ceramics on sale in Chinatown are functional rather than decorative, yet the ceramic shops are worth nosing around for unexpected treasures.

8 Lanterns
In a few of the narrow alleys off Soi Isara Nuphap some families still make traditional Chinese lanterns for a living. Shops along Sampeng Lane sell the finished product in a range of bright colors.

9 Spices
Visitors to any of the fresh markets in Chinatown can admire colorful chili pastes and spices overflowing from huge enamel basins and pick out a few to experiment with at home.

10 Temple Offerings
The most common temple offerings in Bangkok are incense and colored paper, although shops specializing in religious necessities in Chinatown also sell miniature shrines and bright robes to drape around Chinese deities.

See map on pp76–7

Restaurants and Cafés

1 Let The Boy Die
MAP M2 ■ 542 Luang Road ■ (082) 675 9673 ■ Open 6pm–midnight Tue–Sun ■ BB

Enjoy locally brewed craft beer as well as great bistro food, such as gourmet burgers and fish and chips, at this popular eatery.

2 Royal India
MAP D5 ■ 392/1 Chak Phet Road ■ 02 221 6565 ■ Open 10am–10pm daily ■ BB

Set in a back alley, Royal India scores low on decor, but serves diners some great north Indian dishes.

3 Food Center, Old Siam Plaza
MAP C5 ■ Corner of Phahurat ■ Open 10am–5pm daily ■ B

On the third floor of Old Siam Plaza, the food court serves a good range of Thai and Chinese dishes, while the first floor stalls sell Thai desserts.

4 Mandarin Garden
MAP E6 ■ Hotel Royal, 409–21 Yaowarat Rd ■ 02 226 0026 ■ Open 11am–2pm and 5:30–10pm daily ■ BB

The Chinese restaurant in this three-star hotel is famed for its *dim sum*, of which there is a fantastic range. The buffet lunch is a good deal too.

Delicious fare at Shangarila

PRICE CATEGORIES

For a meal for one with one or two dishes and a soft drink, including service.

B under B200   BB B200–1,000
BBB over B1,000

5 Hua Seng Hong
MAP E5 ■ 371–73 Yaowarat Road ■ 02 222 0635 ■ Open 10am–midnight daily ■ BB

Famed for its tasty bird's nest soup, Hua Seng Hong also offers dishes such as *hoy tawt* (mussels in batter).

6 T & K
MAP E6 ■ 49 Soi Phadungdao ■ 02 223 4519 ■ Open 4:30pm–1am Tue–Sun ■ BB

A busy Chinatown restaurant, T & K specializes in barbecued seafood.

7 Hong Kong Noodles
MAP E5 ■ 136 Soi Isara Nuphap ■ Open 10am–8pm daily ■ B

This is a bustling, popular restaurant specializing in roast duck noodles.

8 Chong Kee
MAP F6 ■ 84 Soi Sukon 1, Trimitr Road ■ Open 10am–2pm Mon, 10am–6pm Tue–Sun ■ B

Customers flock here for the house specialty – pork satay on sweet toast.

9 Tep Bar
MAP M3 ■ Soi Nana (near Charoen Krung Road) ■ (09) 8467 2944 ■ Open 5pm–midnight Tue–Sun ■ BB

On artsy Soi Nana, Tep offers delicious food including grilled meats and spicy salads. Also try their Thai herbal whiskey.

10 Shangarila
MAP E5 ■ 306 Yaowarat Road ■ 02 224 5807 ■ Open 10am–10pm daily ■ BB

One of a chain of popular Cantonese restaurants, this huge place serves great fare, including *dim sum*, soups, and stir-fries.

ᴛᴏᴘ10 Downtown

Bangkok's Downtown area radiates out eastward from the Old City and Chinatown. This densely built-up area includes embassies and offices as well as top hotels, restaurants, and entertainment venues. There are a few historical sights, including the Assumption Cathedral, and some gorgeous traditional houses that contrast with all the surrounding skyscrapers. Lush Lumphini Park provides an escape from the concrete jungle, while Silom Road, Siam Square, and Ploenchit are the best shopping areas. Silom is also one of the city's liveliest areas for nightlife; along its infamous side streets, Patpong 1 and 2, market stalls and bars featuring live bands compete with go-go bars for visitors' attention.

Prehistoric pottery, Suan Pakkad

DOWNTOWN

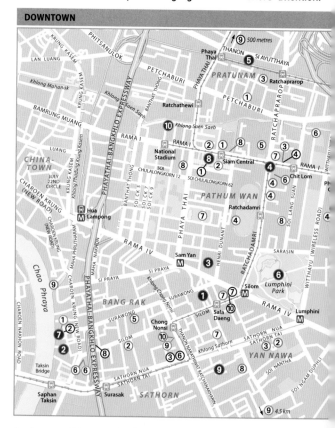

Previous pages A demon guard at the Grand Palace and Wat Phra Kaeo complex

1 Patpong

MAP P5 ▪ Between Silom and Surawong roads ▪ Markets and bars open 6pm–1am daily

Named after a Chinese millionaire who first started to develop these narrow lanes, Patpong 1 and 2 became world famous when their go-go bars were visited by US soldiers on leave from Vietnam in the late 1960s. Its heyday was in the 1980s, during Thailand's first tourist boom. In the early 1990s, a night market was set up along the length of Patpong 1, and the raunchy nightlife began to decline. The downstairs bars include live music cafés and loud go-go bars. Exercise caution at these places, and note that many upstairs bars are rip-off joints.

The elaborate Assumption Cathedral

2 Assumption Cathedral

MAP M6 ▪ Soi Oriental ▪ 02 234 8556 ▪ Open 6am–7pm daily

In quiet backstreets near the river, this imposing building, erected in 1910, replaced a structure from the 1820s. It dominates a tree-lined square that is part of a Catholic mission. The elaborate pink and white exterior matches the bright Rococo interior. The cathedral bears testimony to the success of French missions to Bangkok in the 19th century. While they made few conversions, they managed to secure religious tolerance for all.

3 Snake Farm

MAP P4 ▪ 1871 Rama IV Road ▪ 02 252 0161 ▪ Shows: 2:30pm Mon–Fri, 11am Sat–Sun ▪ Adm

One of Bangkok's quirkier sights, the snake farm is located in the Queen Saovabha Memorial Institute, which was set up in 1923 as the Pasteur Institute. The Thai Red Cross runs it now, producing serums for snake bites and promoting education about snakes. During live demonstrations, snakes are milked of their venom and visitors can have pictures taken with the less harmful varieties.

4 Erawan Shrine

MAP Q3 ■ Corner of Ratchadamri and Ploenchit roads

An island of spirituality in a sea of commerce, the Erawan Shrine is one of Bangkok's quirkiest sights, with the Skytrain zipping by and shopping malls hemming it in. Thailand's most famous spirit house gained its fame in 1956 when its installation was credited with halting a string of fatal accidents at the construction site of the former Erawan Hotel. A constant stream of supplicants offer marigolds, incense, and candles, along with silent wishes.

Erawan Shrine

5 Suan Pakkad

MAP Q1 ■ 352–354 Sri Ayudhya Road ■ 02 246 1775–6 ■ Open 9am–4pm daily ■ Adm ■ www.suanpakkad.com/main_eng.php

This compound of traditional houses was assembled in the 1950s by Prince and Princess Chumbhot on former farmland (the name means "cabbage patch"). The compound has a varied collection of statues, paintings, porcelain, *khon* theater masks, and musical instruments.

6 Lumphini Park

MAP Q4 ■ Corner of Ratchadamri and Rama IV roads ■ Open 5am–8pm daily

It is difficult to imagine how Bangkok might be without this green lung that occupies a huge block in the heart of the commercial and entertainment district. Consisting of a large lake, well-tended lawns, and shady trees, it is busy from dawn with locals walking, jogging, and performing t'ai chi in groups. From February to April, it is a popular site for kite-flying.

7 Oriental Hotel

MAP M5 ■ 48 Oriental Avenue ■ 02 659 9000 ■ www.mandarinoriental.com/bangkok

Bangkok's oldest hotel enjoys double billing as both historic sight and luxurious accommodation option. It has hosted several famous writers, including Joseph Conrad and Somerset Maugham, in the Authors' Wing. Built in 1876, this original part of the hotel is now dwarfed by the Garden and River Wings, but still attracts visitors for afternoon tea in its Authors' Lounge.

8 Siam Square

MAP P2 ■ Corner of Rama I and Phaya Thai roads

Flanked by multistory malls, Siam Square is a grid of streets packed with shopping arcades. The numerous tiny shops, some with no more than a meter frontage, make it a popular shopping area, especially for students from the neighboring Chulalongkorn University, who congregate around Center Point's milk bars and fast-food outlets at the southern end of the square. There are also shops selling designer clothes and fashion accessories, the creation of enterprising young Thai designers, plus a good selection of cafés, restaurants, and cinemas.

The lake at Lumphini Park

M. R. Kukrit's Heritage Home

9 M. R. Kukrit's Heritage Home

MAP P6 ▪ Soi 7, Narathiwat Ratchanakarin Road ▪ 02 286 8185 ▪ **Open** 10am–4pm daily ▪ **Adm**

Descended from Rama II *(see p33)*, Mom Rajawongse Kukrit Pramoj (1911–95) was one of the best-loved Thais of the 20th century. He founded the newspaper *Siam Rath* and wrote hundreds of plays, poems, and novels. He even served as Prime Minister in 1975–6. His house, with many beautiful artworks and a garden, is preserved as he left it.

BANGKOK TRAFFIC

Traffic in Bangkok is known for going nowhere. Drivers sit in a sea of vehicles. Yet it was not always like this. In *The Land of the White Elephant* (1873), Frank Vincent writes: "the nobles...may occasionally be seen taking a drive at the fashionable hour of the afternoon, sitting gravely upright and...looking upon their friends...with a sense of new-found importance."

10 Jim Thompson House

One of the most popular sights in Bangkok, this beautiful compound of traditional Thai houses set in a lush tropical garden allows visitors to imagine how life in a well-to-do, mid-20th century Bangkok home might have been. The evocative furnishings, sculptures, and tapestries give the building a refined character. Visitors to the house must join a guided tour, which are regular and in several languages *(see pp30–31)*.

A WALK THROUGH THE OLD FARANG QUARTER

▶ **MORNING**

Begin this half-mile (1-km) walking tour at the upscale **River City Shopping Complex** *(see p61)*, on the riverfront just north of the pier at Tha Si Phraya. You will find jewelry, books, restaurants, clothes, and more. On the third and fourth floor are shops selling rare antiques, and an antiques auction is held every fourth Saturday of the month. From here head back south, passing the **Royal Orchid Sheraton** *(see p114)* and the **Portuguese Embassy**. Operational from 1820, this was the first embassy to be established in Siam by any European power. Follow the lane out to Charoen Krung Road and turn right to reach the **General Post Office**, a massive Art Deco building. Walk south along Charoen Krung from the post office and turn right into Soi 34 to see old wooden houses; the winding lane leads to **Haroon Mosque**, a small, attractive stucco building used by the local Muslim population. The next lane south, Soi 36, is home to the **French Embassy**, which was the second embassy to be established in Bangkok. Walk south, crossing Soi 38 and 40 to reach the **Assumption Cathedral** *(see p85)*. From the cathedral, follow an alley west towards the river, where the former headquarters of the East Asiatic Company, built in 1901, still stands. Have tea and cakes in the Authors' Lounge at the historic **Oriental Hotel** *(see p85)* next door to end your morning's walk.

See map on pp84–5 ←

The Best of the Rest

1 Pratunam Market
MAP Q1 ▪ Corner of Phetburi and Ratchaprarop roads ▪ Open 9am–midnight daily

Famous for its inexpensive textiles and ready-made clothes, Pratunam Market is a great place to witness the city's chaotic street life.

2 Maha Uma Devi Temple
MAP N5 ▪ Corner of Silom Road and Soi Pan ▪ 02 238 4007 ▪ Open 6am–8pm daily

Also known as Sri Mariamman, this temple features a panoply of brightly painted Hindu deities above the entrance and around the interior walls.

Statue at Maha Uma Devi

3 Baiyoke Tower II
MAP Q1 ▪ 222 Ratchaprarop Road ▪ 02 656 3000 ▪ Open 10am–11pm daily ▪ Adm

Bangkok's second-tallest building at 1,000 ft (304 m), this tower has an open-air, revolving roof deck that offers superb panoramas of the city.

4 Royal Bangkok Sports Club
MAP Q3 ▪ Henri Dunant Road ▪ 02 652 5000 ▪ www.rbsc.org

This attractive horse-racing club has a golf course set inside the track.

5 Neilson Hays Library
MAP N5 ▪ 195 Suriwong Road ▪ 02 233 1731 ▪ Open 9:30am–5pm Tue–Sun

Located in a colonial building, this haven for bookworms has over 20,000 volumes on its shelves.

6 Chao Mae Tubtim Shrine
MAP R2 ▪ Wireless Road

This eye-catching shrine is encircled by phallic offerings from devotees wishing for fertility or prosperity.

7 Chulalongkorn University
MAP P3 ▪ 254 Phaya Thai Road ▪ 02 215 0871 ▪ www.chula.ac.th

The campus of Thailand's oldest and most respected university mixes Western and Thai architectural styles.

8 SEA LIFE Bangkok Ocean World
MAP P2 ▪ Basement, Siam Paragon, Rama I Road ▪ 02 687 2000 ▪ Open 10am–9pm daily ▪ Adm ▪ www.sealifebangkok.com

This massive aquarium, home to over 400 species of marine life, features an underwater tunnel (see p55).

9 Museum of Counterfeit Goods
MAP T6 ▪ Tilleke & Gibbins, Supalai Grand Tower, Rama III Road ▪ 02 056 5546 ▪ Open by appointment

Quirky displays of over 4,000 fake items, including clothing and drugs.

10 Mahanakhon Building
MAP P5 ▪ Narathiwat Ratchanakharin Road

Currently Thailand's tallest building, with a rooftop bar and observatory planned for late 2017.

Mahanakhon Building

Shopping Malls

1 Siam Paragon
MAP P2 ■ Rama I Road, Siam Square ■ 02 690 1000 ■ Open 10am–10pm daily ■ www.siamparagon.co.th
With six floors of designer boutiques, bookshops, cinemas, restaurants, and fitness centers, this mall is one of the most popular in Bangkok.

2 Siam Center and Siam Discovery Center
MAP P2 ■ 989 Rama I Road ■ 02 658 1000 ■ Open 10am–10pm daily
Known for designer brands, trendy shops, and restaurants, these two adjoining malls attract young adults. Look out for local fashion labels such as Greyhound, Baking Soda, and Theatre.

3 Narai Phand
MAP Q2 ■ President Tower, 973 Ploenchit Road ■ 02 656 0398 ■ Open 10am–8pm daily
At this government-sponsored shop for promoting quality Thai handicrafts, everything is sold at fixed prices: woodcarvings, lacquerware, silk clothing, silverware, and more.

4 Peninsula Plaza
MAP Q3 ■ 153 Ratchadamri Road ■ 02 253 9791 ■ Open 10am–8pm daily
This mall consists mostly of jewelers and designer outlets.

5 CentralWorld
MAP Q2 ■ 4/1–2 Ratchadamri Road ■ 02 640 7000 ■ Open 10am–10pm daily ■ www.centralworld.co.th
Huge shopping complex with fashion boutiques, jewelers, home decor outlets, a bowling alley, and cinemas.

6 Erawan Bangkok
MAP Q3 ■ 494 Ploenchit Road ■ 02 250 7777 ■ Open 10am–9pm daily ■ www.erawanbangkok.com
Next to the Erawan Shrine, this luxury mall has plenty of boutiques by famous names, as well as classy cafés and a wellness center.

The stylish Gaysorn Plaza

7 Gaysorn Plaza
MAP Q2 ■ Ploenchit Road ■ 02 656 1149 ■ Open 10am–8pm daily
Successful young Thai designers display their wares here.

8 Mahboonkrong (MBK)
MAP P3 ■ Phaya Thai Road ■ Open 10am–10pm daily ■ www.mbk-center.co.th
Packed with five floors of fashions, accessories, electronics, cosmetics, jewelry, and eateries, MBK feels like a cross between a street market and a shopping mall (see p60).

9 EmQuartier
MAP T6 ■ 693 Sukhumvit Road ■ 02 269 1188 ■ Open 10am–10pm daily ■ www.emporium.co.th
Across the street from the Emporium, this mall has a less formal atmosphere and many boutiques.

10 Emporium
MAP T6 ■ 622 Sukhumvit Road ■ 02 269 1000 ■ Open 10am–10pm daily ■ www.emporium.co.th
An upscale mall, Emporium features a department store, designer boutiques, restaurants, and cafés.

See map on pp84–5

Ways to Enjoy the River

1 Chao Phraya Express Boats

chaophrayaexpressboat.com
This extensive public transport system is both picturesque and useful. There are several color-coded routes, and the website explains everything.

2 Loy Nava Cruise

MAP M5 ■ Si Phraya Pier ■ 02 437 4932 ■ Cruise 6–8pm and 8–10pm ■ www.loynava.com ■ BBB

Choose from traditional, seafood, and vegetarian Thai dishes, then sit back and enjoy the fare on this rice barge as it chugs up and down the Chao Phraya River.

3 Anantara Sleep-on-Board Cruise to Ayutthaya

bangkok-cruises.anantara.com
The Anantara hotel group offers luxurious three-day cruises up the Chao Phraya to Ayutthaya, with accommodation aboard their lavishly refurbished teak rice barges. Although this is an expensive trip, it is a memorable experience.

Anantara sleep-on-board cruise

4 Canal Tours

These can be arranged with a tour agency or by negotiating with the boat captains directly. Good stops are the Royal Barge Museum (see p96) and the artist's village at Khlong Bang Luang (see p62).

5 Hotel and Other Free Shuttles

Just west of the BTS Saphan Taksin station, take a shuttle voyage to one of the spectacular riverside hotels on the Thonburi bank – such as the Millennium Hilton or the Anantara – for a meal or drink.

6 Charter Long-Tail Boat to Ko Kret

At any riverside pier, enterprising long-tail boat captains offer their vessels for hire. If you have a group of four or more, a visit to Ko Kret (see p95) would make for an excellent day trip. Agree a price, and pay upon returning to your point of origin.

7 Manohra Cruise

MAP S6 ■ Anantara Bangkok Riverside Pier ■ 02 476 0022 ■ Cruise 7:30–9:30pm ■ www.manohra cruises.com ■ BBB

Operating out of the Anantara Bangkok Riverside, this cruise offers guests tasty curries and stir-fries.

8 Pearl of Siam Cruise

MAP M5 ■ River City Pier ■ 02 861 0255 ■ Cruise 7:30–9:30pm ■ www.grandpearlcruise.com ■ BBB

This cruise is perfect for those looking for a lively evening. Boats are big and offer live music and lounge areas, plus a blowout buffet.

9 Public Water Taxis to Bang Krajao

This oasis of clean air and greenery (see p97) can be reached by a public boat from behind Wat Khlong Toey Nok or by chartering a private long-tail from anywhere on the river.

10 Yok Yor Cruise

MAP L4 ■ 885 Somdet Chaophraya 17 Road ■ 02 863 0565 ■ Cruise 8–10pm ■ www.yokyor.co.th/cruise/index.html ■ BB

Bangkok's only budget dinner cruise is popular but the menu is limited.

Restaurants

PRICE CATEGORIES

For a meal for one with one or two dishes and a soft drink, including service.

B under B200　　BB B200–1,000
BBB over B1,000

1 Le Normandie

MAP M5 ■ Mandarin Oriental Hotel, 48 Oriental Avenue ■ 02 659 9000 ■ Open noon–2pm & 7–10pm Mon–Sat ■ www.mandarinoriental.com/bangkok ■ BBB

The Brittany lobster and pan-fried duck liver are specialties of this French restaurant.

2 Ban Khun Mae

MAP P2 ■ 458/7–9 Siam Square Soi 8 ■ 02 658 4112 ■ Open 11am–11pm daily ■ BB

With its extensive menu of classic Thai dishes, Ban Khun Mae is an ideal spot for lunch or dinner.

3 Rong Mahal

MAP T6 ■ Rembrandt Hotel, 26th floor, Sukhumvit Soi 18 ■ 02 261 7100 ■ Open 6pm–midnight daily, & 11am–2:30pm Sun ■ BB

Consistently named Bangkok's best Indian restaurant, Rong Mahal serves elegant, authentic Northern Indian cuisine and has great views.

4 Liu

MAP R3 ■ Conrad Hotel, 87 Wireless Road ■ 02 690 9999 ■ Open 11:30am–2:30pm & 6–10:30pm daily ■ BBB

This elegant gourmet Chinese restaurant serves classic regional cuisines – Cantonese, Shanghainese, Sichuan – with a contemporary twist.

5 Lenzi Tuscan Kitchen

MAP Q3 ■ Ruam Rudee Soi 2 ■ 02 001 0116 ■ Open 11:45am–2pm, 6–10:45pm daily ■ BBB

A chef famous for several Italian restaurants focuses here on his native Tuscany. Some of the produce is from the family farm near Pisa.

6 Breeze

MAP M6 ■ 52nd floor, State Tower, 1055 Silom Road ■ 02 624 9555 ■ Open 6pm–midnight daily ■ BBB

Come here for spectacular views and impeccable (but pricey) Asian food.

Incredible food and views at Breeze

7 Eat Me

MAP P5 ■ Soi Pipat 2, Convent Road ■ 02 238 0931 ■ Open 3pm–1am daily ■ BB

A very imaginative international fusion menu is offered here.

8 Gaggan

MAP Q3 ■ 68/1 Soi Langsuan (opp Soi 3) ■ 02 652 1700 ■ Open 6–11pm daily ■ BBB

Gaggan serves progressive Indian food unlike any you've eaten before.

9 L'Atelier de Joël Robuchon

MAP P5 ■ MahaNakhon CUBE, 5th floor, Narathiwat Ratchanakarin Road ■ 02 001 0698 ■ Open 11:30am–2pm & 6:30–10pm daily ■ BBB

French haute cuisine is served in an informal setting. Robuchon has been called "chef of the century."

10 Issaya Siamese Club

MAP off R6 ■ 4 Soi Sri Aksorn, Chua Ploeng Road ■ 02 672 9040–1 ■ Open 11:30am–2:30pm & 6–10:30pm daily ■ BB

Excellent Thai cuisine is served in a former mansion with a lovely garden.

See map on pp84–5

Bars and Pubs

1 Diplomat Bar
MAP R3 ■ Conrad Hotel, All Seasons Place, 87 Wireless Road (Witthayu) ■ 02 690 9999 ■ Open 7am–1am Sun–Thu, 7am–2am Fri & Sat

Unwind along with the high-flyers at this super-elegant bar while sipping a cocktail and enjoying the resident jazz band.

2 The Zuk Bar
MAP Q5 ■ Sukhothai Hotel, 13/3 South Sathorn Road ■ 02 344 8888 ■ Open 5pm–1am Mon–Sat, 5pm–midnight Sun ■ www.sukhothai.com

A relaxing place for drinks at the end of a hot day, accompanied by Thai tapas, Japanese grilled skewers, and sushi – even more appealing during Happy Hour (until 8pm).

3 Moon Bar
MAP Q6 ■ Banyan Tree Hotel, South Sathorn Road ■ 02 679 1200 ■ Open 5pm–1am daily

Enjoy the fabulous views from high up above the city at Moon Bar, which offers a complete range of cocktails.

4 Bar@494
MAP Q3 ■ 494 Ratchadamri Road ■ 02 254 1234 ■ Open 3pm–midnight daily

The excellent wines and tapas are reasonably priced at this small bar in the Grand Hyatt.

5 Oskar Bistro
MAP T6 ■ 24 Sukhumvit Soi 11 ■ 02 255 3377 ■ Open 4pm–2am daily

Great for a pre- or post-clubbing drink and snack, this stylish place has good craft beers and cocktails.

6 Sky Bar
MAP M6 ■ 63rd floor, State Tower, 1055 Silom Road ■ 02 624 9555 ■ Open 6pm–1am daily

Indulge in a pricey sundowner at the Sky Bar and admire the view from near the top of the State Tower.

7 Flann O'Brien's
MAP P5 ■ 62/1-2 Silom Road ■ 02 632 7515 ■ Open 9am–1am daily

The Irish theme at this pub includes Guinness on tap, and has Irish lamb stew on the menu.

8 Small's
MAP Q6 ■ 186/3 Suan Phlu Soi 1 ■ (09) 5585 1398 ■ Open 8:30pm–2am Wed–Mon

Come here for the city's best whiskey selection. Light meals are served while jazz plays in the background.

9 Viva & Aviv The River
MAP M5 ■ Ground floor, River City shopping centre ■ 02 639 6305 ■ Open 11am–midnight daily

Wonderful cocktails, comfort food and a lovely river terrace are high-lights of this riverside bar.

10 Hyde and Seek
MAP R3 ■ Athenée Residence, 65/1 Soi Ruam Rudee ■ 02 168 5152 ■ Open 4:30pm–1am daily

A classy but lively gastrobar, with plenty of appealing garden seating, and DJs every night.

Amazing views at Moon Bar

Nightclubs and Music Venues

Ever-popular Hard Rock Café

(1) Hard Rock Café
MAP P3 ▪ 424/3–6 Soi 11, Siam Square ▪ 02 658 4090 ▪ Open 11:30am–1am daily

With a formula that has been tried and tested worldwide, this is one of the city's liveliest night spots (see p56).

(2) Bamboo Bar
A brilliant spot for jazz lovers, Bamboo Bar has an excellent resident band, an elegant tropical atmosphere, and attentive waitresses who ensure they keep the drinks flowing (see p56).

(3) WOOBAR®
MAP P6 ▪ W Bangkok Hotel, 106 North Sathorn Road ▪ 02 344 4000 ▪ Open 9am–midnight daily

A variety of sounds, from techno to funky house, are played at this beautifully sophisticated hotel bar.

(4) Mixx Discotheque
MAP Q2 ▪ President Tower Arcade, 973 Phloen Chit Road ▪ 02 656 0383 ▪ Open 10pm–2am daily ▪ Adm

Known for its superb acoustics and sound system, this club plays hip-hop, R&B, and house music.

(5) Levels
MAP T6 ▪ Aloft Hotel, 6th floor, Sukhumvit Soi 11 ▪ (08) 2308 3246 ▪ Open 9pm–3am daily

Different styles of music play in each of this hot club's three party zones, which include a chill-out lounge bar.

(6) Ce La Vi
MAP N6 ▪ Sathorn Square Complex, 98 North Sathorn Road ▪ 02 108 2000 ▪ Open 9pm–2am Tue–Sat ▪ Adm on weekends

Downtown's most elegant dancing spot occupies the two top floors of a skyscraper. The music varies nightly.

(7) DJ Station
MAP P5 ▪ Silom Soi 2 ▪ 02 266 4029 ▪ Open 10pm–2am daily ▪ Adm

Silom Soi 2 is dominated by gay clubs, and this three-floor nightclub is the most popular.

(8) Maggie Choo's
MAP M5 ▪ Novotel Bangkok Fenix Silom Hotel, 320 Silom Road ▪ 091 772 2144 ▪ Open 7pm–2am daily

One of Bangkok's most imaginative nightspots, this has 1930s decor, live jazz, and good food on offer.

Jazz band at Maggie Choo's

(9) Saxophone
MAP T6 ▪ 3/8 Phaya Thai Road ▪ 02 245 3592 ▪ Open 6pm–2am daily

A Bangkok music institution for 30 years, Saxophone offers live jazz, blues, and reggae. It's a friendly spot that is also popular with locals for its excellent Thai food.

(10) Tapas
MAP P5 ▪ Soi 4, Silom Road ▪ 02 656 4249 ▪ Open 7pm–2am daily

The city's best small club, playing mostly house music, Tapas has pavement seating to relax in.

See map on pp84–5

🔟 Greater Bangkok

Most of Bangkok's suburban areas are housing estates, but there are also some unmissable sights, like Chatuchak Weekend Market. The former capital Thonburi has the enigmatic Wat Arun and the Royal Barge Museum. To the north of the Old City, Dusit features the magnificent Dusit Park *(see pp22–3)*. East of the city lie Kamthieng House and the Rama IX Royal Park, while a short boat ride north, Nonthaburi and Koh Kret offer a taste of provincial Thailand.

Riverside Wat Arun temple

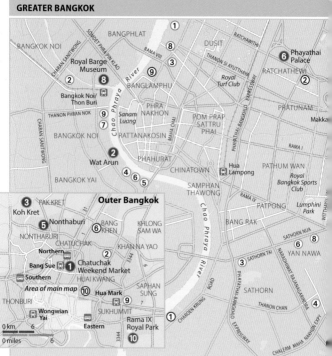

GREATER BANGKOK

1 Chatuchak Weekend Market

This market covers a massive area, with about 15,000 stalls selling a mind-boggling range of products, from plants and animals to antiques and paintings. Considered to be the world's largest open-air market, Chatuchak is too big to see everything in a day, so pick up a map at the entrance and target the areas that interest you *(see pp28–9)*.

2 Wat Arun

This ancient temple in Thonburi, on the west bank of the Chao Phraya River, is one of Bangkok's best-known icons with its five *prangs* (towers). These *prangs* are covered with broken shards of colorful porcelain that create an intriguing abstract pattern when viewed up close. The temple's

bot (ordination hall) is also worth exploring, both for its murals and the exquisite Buddha image, which was apparently molded by King Rama II *(see p33)*.

3 Koh Kret

MAP S4 ■ 4 miles (7 km) N of Nonthaburi

Combining a trip to Nonthaburi with an exploration of Koh Kret, an ox-bow island in a meander of the Chao Phraya River, makes for an enjoyable day. Hire a longtail boat from Nonthaburi to reach Koh Kret. The island is inhabited by the Mon people, who make terra-cotta pots for sale in markets in the city. There are no cars, so you can listen to the twitter of birds as you wander around the island, passing mango, papaya, and durian plantations, pausing to watch busy potters at work, and perhaps picking up a sample of their work.

Temple on the island of Koh Kret

4 Soi Thonglor

MAP T6

Also known as Sukhumvit Soi 55, this area of east Bangkok is popular with young Thai professionals and expats. There's nothing of great cultural significance here, but the area has a fun vibe, with many restaurants, bars, and boutiques. Take BTS to Thonglor station, stroll a mile (1.6 km) up one side of the street and return on the other, taking in the lively cafés and entertainment venues.

Map legend

- ① Top 10 Sights
  see pp94–7
- ① Restaurants
  see p99
- ① Best of the Rest
  see p98
- ① Bars and Pubs
  see p100
- ① Nightclubs and Entertainment
  see p101

DIN DAENG

MAHANAKHON EXPY

SIRAT EXPRESSWAY

Benchakitti Park

RATCHADAPHISEK RD

SUKHUMVIT ROAD

Kamthieng House

KHLONG TAN NUEA

Soi Thonglor

WATTHANA

Eastern

RAMA IV

PHRA KHANONG

CHALERM MAHANAKHON EXPRESSWAY

Chao Phraya River

⑨ Bang Krajao

0 kilometers   1.5
0 miles   1.5

Fruit and vegetable vendors spread out their produce in Nonthaburi market

⑤ Nonthaburi

MAP S4 ■ Nonthaburi Province

Take the express ferry heading north from any pier in the city center and get off at the last stop in Nonthaburi. Here, the Wat Chalerm Phra Kiet temple, originally built by Rama III (see p33), features intricate porcelain tilework on the doors and window frames of the *bot* (ordination hall). This region is famed for the superior quality of its durian fruit.

Phayathai Palace's cone-topped turret

⑥ Phayathai Palace

MAP H1 ■ Ratchawithi Road ■ 02 354 7987 ■ Tours 1pm Tue & Thu, 9:30am and 1:30pm Sat & Sun

This palace was built in 1909 as a royal country retreat. After the 1932 coup (see p40), it was commandeered by the Thai military as a hospital (Phramongkutklao Hospital), which still functions around the palace today. The highlight of the palace is the Thewaratsaparom Throne Hall, which has beautifully carved pillars, balconies, and archways.

⑦ Kamthieng House

MAP T6 ■ 131 Sukhumvit Soi 21 ■ 02 661 6470–3 ■ Open 9am–5pm Tue–Sat ■ www.siam-society.org

This beautiful Lanna house began life in the mid-19th century as the home of the Nimman-heimin family in Chiang Mai, but was carefully dismantled and reconstructed on this site in 1962 when it was donated to the Siam Society. Today it functions as an ethnological museum, with farming implements, a multi-media display on the Thai belief in spirits, a rural kitchen, and a granary with an exhibition on rice-farming rituals.

⑧ Royal Barge Museum

MAP A2 ■ Khlong Bangkok Noi ■ 02 424 0004 ■ Open 9am–5pm daily ■ Adm

This display of vessels offers a glimpse into the pageantry of the Thai monarchy. On rare ceremonial occasions, the elaborately decorated barges are propelled by bedecked oarsmen. The main barge on display, *Suphannahongse*, carries the Thai King and Queen at such times. It is carved out of a single teak tree. Its prow is adorned with a majestic golden swan.

⑨ Bang Krajao

MAP T6 ▪ MRT to Khlong Toey, then taxi to pier behind Wat Khlong Toey Nok

Cycling is a great way to see this area, an oasis of traditional villages, mangrove forests, and fruit orchards on the west side of the Chao Phraya River. Bicycles can be hired at the pier. Nearby, the Sri Nakhon Kuenkhan Park has huge trees, landscaped gardens, and pavilions on a lake.

THE DREADED DURIAN

The durian, a most unusual fruit, arouses adoration and disgust in equal measure for its strong repelling smell and heavenly creamy taste. The spiky shell belies the soft yellow pods beneath it, cushioned by thick padding. The mushy texture and smooth, tangy taste take some getting used to, but once hooked there is no going back.

⑩ Rama IX Royal Park

MAP U6 ▪ Sukhumvit Soi 103 ▪ Open 5am–6pm daily ▪ Adm

This is an ideal spot to head for when you need a break from Bangkok's relentless congestion. Though it takes a while to get to the park, on entering the 200 acre (81 hectare) site, the effort becomes worthwhile. The park was opened in 1987 to commemorate the 60th birthday of Rama IX (see p41), and contains a museum explaining the life and achievements of the king, a large lake with pedal boats, as well as beautifully landscaped grounds with several unusual plants that are clearly labeled.

Rama IX Royal Park

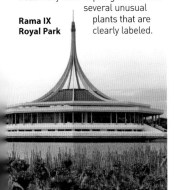

Chatuchak Weekend Market — Mo Chit Skytrain Station — Royal Barge Museum — Tha Thien — Wat Arun — FERRY — SKYTRAIN — Saphan Taksin

▶ MORNING

Start before 8am and make your way to Mo Chit Skytrain station for a good look round **Chatuchak Weekend Market** (see pp28–9). Pick up a map at the main entrance on the Phaholyothin Road and go straight ahead through the maze of stalls to the slender clocktower to orient yourself. Check out section 8 (handicrafts), wander through sections 9–15 (pets and accessories) before stocking up your wardrobe in sections 10–21 (clothing and footwear). As there are thousands of foodstalls, you can refuel whenever you get hungry or thirsty.

AFTERNOON

At midday, return to Mo Chit station and take the Skytrain to Saphan Taksin. From here, take an express ferry upriver to Tha Tien, then hop on one of the regular cross-river ferries to **Wat Arun** (see pp32–3). Take a good look at the bright ceramics on the prangs (towers), and clamber up the steep steps of the central spire for a panoramic river view. Rest in a breezy riverside pavilion before taking the ferry back to Tha Tien. Get some refreshment at **Rub Aroon** café, just around the corner (see p75), then take an express boat to Phra Pinklao pier, which is a ten-minute walk from the **Royal Barge Museum**: head up the road and take the first left down Soi Wat Dusitaram. Marvel over the intricate decoration of the other-worldly vessels on display here before heading back to your base.

See map on pp94–5

The Best of the Rest

1 Christian Churches
MAP S5 ■ S of Ratchawithi Road

Near the riverbank in Dusit district are three churches built for resident foreigners: St. Francis Xavier Church with its mainly Vietnamese congregation, the Church of the Immaculate Conception, which was established by French missionaries, and a small Cambodian Church.

Mural at Wat Suwannaram

2 Wat Suwannaram
MAP S5 ■ 33 Charan Sanit Wong Soi 32 ■ 02 433 8045 ■ Open 8am–5pm daily

This temple is home to superb murals depicting episodes from the *Jataka Tales*, which tell the story of the Buddha's previous lives.

3 Wat Indrawiharn
MAP D1 ■ 144 Wisut Kasat Road ■ 02 281 1406 ■ Open 6am–6pm daily

The main attraction of this temple tucked away in the backstreets of Dusit is the 105-ft (32-m) tall standing Buddha.

4 Wat Kalayanamit
MAP B6 ■ Soi Wat Kanlaya ■ Open 8am–5pm daily

The country's largest indoor sitting Buddha (50 ft/15 m) and its biggest bronze bell are both found here.

5 Wat Prayun
MAP C6 ■ Pratchatipok Road ■ Open 8am–6pm daily

An artificial hill covered with *chedis* (stupas) and shrines is the highlight at Wat Prayun. Devotees release turtles in the pond nearby.

6 Church of Santa Cruz
MAP C6 ■ Soi Kudi Chin ■ Open 5–8pm Mon–Sat, 9am–8pm Sun

This church was built by the Portuguese in 1782. The present building, with its pastel colors and octagonal dome, dates back to 1913.

7 Wat Rakhang
MAP A4 ■ Soi Wat Rakhang

A little-visited temple, Wat Rakhang has a wooden scripture library behind the *bot* (ordination hall), where there are murals from the days when Rama I (r.1782–1809) lived here as a monk.

8 Thewet Flower Market
MAP D1 ■ Krung Kasem Road ■ Open 9am–6pm daily

With its bright blooms, sweet scent in the air, and the friendly smiles of the vendors, this canalside market is an appealing place to explore.

9 Prasart Museum
MAP U6 ■ 9 Krungthep Kreetha Soi 4A ■ 02 379 3601 ■ Open 9am–2pm Tue–Sun by appointment ■ Adm

Set in a landscaped garden, this museum features artworks housed in reproductions of famous buildings.

10 Bangkok Dolls Museum
This museum displays dolls from around the world, all dressed in miniature costumes and presented in context *(see p54)*.

Restaurants

PRICE CATEGORIES

For a meal for one with one or two dishes and a soft drink, including service.

B under B200   **BB** B200–1,000
BBB over B1,000

1 Bo.Lan
MAP T6 ■ 24 Sukhumvit Soi 53 ■ 02 260 2962 ■ Open 6–10:30pm Tue–Sun, plus noon–2:30pm Sat & Sun ■ BB

Set in a beautiful wooden house near Soi Thonglor, Bo.Lan serves authentic but unusual Thai cuisine.

2 Le Dalat
MAP T6 ■ 57 Soi Prasanmitr, Sukhumvit 23 ■ 02 259 9593 ■ 11:30am–2:30pm & 5:30–10:30pm daily ■ BB

Bangkok's top Vietnamese restaurant serves diners a host of exquisitely prepared traditional dishes.

3 Blue Elephant
MAP N6 ■ 233 South Sathorn Road ■ 02 673 9353–8 ■ Open 11:30am–2:30pm & 6–10:30pm daily ■ www.blueelephant.com ■ BBB

Set in a stunning century-old building, the Blue Elephant specializes in Royal Thai Cuisine.

4 Le Lys
MAP T6 ■ 148/11 Nang Linchi Soi 6 ■ 02 287 1898 ■ Open 5–10:30pm Mon–Fri, 11am–10:30pm Sat–Sun ■ www.lelys.info ■ BB

This restaurant serves traditional Thai food without making it too spicy, to suit Western palates.

5 Cabbages & Condoms
MAP T6 ■ 6–8 Sukhumvit Soi 12 ■ 02 229 4610 ■ Open 11am–10pm daily ■ BB

Reasonable prices make this place a good choice, and all proceeds go toward AIDS prevention programs.

6 Baan Khanitha
MAP T6 ■ 69 South Sathorn Road ■ 02 675 4200–1 ■ Open 11am–11pm daily ■ www.baan-khanitha.com ■ BB

One of the city's oldest upscale eateries serves classic Thai dishes.

Upmarket restaurant Baan Khanitha

7 Indus
MAP T6 ■ 71 Sukhumvit Soi 26 ■ 02 258 4900 ■ Open 11:30am–2:30pm & 6pm–midnight daily ■ BB

Indus serves contemporary Indian vegetarian and meat dishes.

8 Celadon
MAP Q5 ■ Sukhothai Hotel, 13/3 South Sathorn Road ■ 02 344 8888 ■ Open noon–3pm & 6:30–11pm daily ■ BBB

This award-winning restaurant serves sublime Thai food. The lotus pond completes the scene.

Thai food at Celadon

9 Supatra River House
MAP A4 ■ 266 Soi Wat Rakhang ■ 02 411 0305 ■ Open 11:30am–2:30pm & 5:30–11pm daily ■ BB

Excellent seafood and great riverside views at this restaurant.

10 Basil
MAP T6 ■ Sheraton Grande Sukhumvit, 250 Sukhumvit Road ■ 02 649 8366 ■ Open noon–2:30pm & 6–10:30pm Mon–Fri & Sun, 6–10:30pm Sat ■ BBB

Diners can savor delicious Thai dishes in sophisticated surroundings.

See map on pp94–5

Bars and Pubs

1 Mikkeller Bangkok
MAP T6 ▪ 26 Yaek 2, Soi 10, Soi Ekamai, Sukhumvit Road ▪ 02 381 9891 ▪ Open 5pm–midnight daily

Located in a suburban house, this branch of the famous Danish micro-brewery offers 30 craft beers from around the world on tap.

2 Fat Gutz Saloon
MAP U5 ▪ Central Eastville, Chalong Rat Expressway ▪ 099 161 3951 ▪ Open 10:30am–1am daily

This place has quite a chic, upmarket clientele. There's a shipboard theme, with incredible cocktails, fish and chips, and live blues performances.

Stunning skyline views at Octave

3 Octave Rooftop Lounge Bar
MAP T6 ▪ Marriott Sukhumvit, 45th floor, Sukhumvit Soi 57 ▪ 02 797 0000 ▪ Open 5pm–2am daily

One of the best rooftop bars in the city, with 360-degree views, Octave is perfect for a sunset drink before dinner and clubbing on Soi Thonglor.

4 Nest at Le Fenix Hotel
MAP T6 ▪ 33 Sukhumvit Soi 11 ▪ 02 255 0638–9 ▪ Open 6pm–2am daily

Sofas and rattan beds are dotted about this bar set in stylish rooftop gardens. A retractable roof comes in handy during rainstorms.

5 Zanzibar
MAP T6 ▪ 139 Sukhumvit Soi 11 ▪ 02 651 2700 ▪ Open 9am–2am daily

Set in a lovely garden, this Italian bar and restaurant has been a hit since day one. There is a live jazz band here every night.

6 Long Table
MAP T6 ▪ 25th floor, 48 Column Tower, Sukhumvit Road, Soi 16 ▪ 02 302 2557 ▪ Open 5pm–2am daily

There are exceptional views over the city from the balconies of this achingly fashionable restaurant and bar which has an extensive food menu as well.

7 Tuba
MAP T6 ▪ 30 Soi 21, Sukhumvit Road, Soi 63 ▪ 02 711 5500 ▪ Open 11am–2am daily

A second-hand furniture shop and restaurant by day; by night a place to play pool and listen to some 70s tunes.

8 Black Swan
MAP T6 ▪ Sukhumvit Soi 19 ▪ 02 229 4542 ▪ Open 8am–1am daily

As the name suggests, this is a British-style pub offering a range of imported beers and generous portions of typical pub food.

9 Studio Lam
MAP T6 ▪ Soi 51, Sukhumvit Road ▪ 02 261 6661 ▪ Open 6pm–1am Tue–Sun

DJs play great Thai folk and world music every night at this cozy and friendly neighborhood bar.

10 WTF
MAP T6 ▪ 7 Soi 51, Sukhumvit Road ▪ 02 662 6246 ▪ Open 6pm–1am Tue–Sun

A cool, Spanish-influenced bar that doubles as an art gallery, WTF offers great tapas, cocktails, and wines.

Nightclubs and Entertainment

Elaborate dance performance at Calypso Cabaret

1 Calypso Cabaret
MAP S6 ▪ Asiatique the Riverfront, 2194 Charoen Krung 72–76 Road ▪ 02 688 1415 ▪ Show 8:15pm, 9:45pm daily ▪ Adm ▪ www.calypsocabaret.com

Transvestites in sequins lip-synch and dance to pop songs *(see p51)*.

2 Saxophone
Moderate prices and great music bring both Thais and foreigners to Saxophone *(see p56)*.

3 The Iron Fairies
MAP T6 ▪ 402 Soi Thonglor ▪ 02 714 8875 or 09 9918 1600 ▪ Open 6pm–2am daily

Like a cross between an Edwardian factory and a magical playground. Enjoy great burgers as you listen to live jazz. Book a table in advance.

4 Clouds
MAP T6 ▪ G/F Seenspace, 251/1 Thonglor Soi 13 ▪ 02 185 2365 ▪ Open 5pm–2am daily

This very hip Thonglor dance spot plays mainly funky electronica and offers the best pizza in Bangkok.

5 Tawandang German Brewery
MAP T6 ▪ 462/61 Narathiwat Ratchanakharin ▪ 02 678 1114–5 ▪ Open 5pm–1am daily

Get a big helping of home-brewed beer while big bands play *morlam* music from northeast Thailand.

6 Lumphini Stadium
MAP T4 ▪ Ram Intra Road ▪ Fights 6:30pm Tue & Fri, 4pm Sat & Sun

Bangkok's second major Thai boxing stadium moved out to the suburbs near Don Muang Airport in 2014.

7 Titanium Bar
MAP T6 ▪ Sukhumvit Soi 22 ▪ 02 258 3758 ▪ Open 8pm–2am daily

Featuring an ice bar, the cool but unpretentious Titanium hosts "the best all-girl rock band in Thailand." They play mostly covers but really know how to make it swing.

8 Living Room
MAP T6 ▪ Sheraton Grande Sukhumvit, 250 Sukhumvit Road ▪ 02 649 8888 ▪ Open 9am–midnight daily

A stylish hang-out with a sophisticated ambience, Living Room features top class jazz musicians every evening and at Sunday lunch.

9 Adhere the 13th
This club may be small, but the combination of a band, cheap beer, and friendly vibe make it a popular hangout *(see p56)*.

10 Siam Niramit
One of the largest stage productions in the world, featuring over 150 performers, 500 costumes, and lots of special effects that take the audience on a spectacular journey to the enchanted kingdom of Thailand *(see p50)*.

See map on pp94–5

🔟 Beyond Bangkok

Bangkok's sights are liable to cause sensory overload, from the dazzling temples to the constant crowds. Fortunately, when visitors feel they need a break, there are plenty of opportunities for a day trip or an overnight stay away from the city. Tour operators can arrange undemanding and entertaining trips to nearby attractions, such as the Floating Market and the Ancient City. For an excursion with more cultural content, head for the ruins of Ayutthaya, the country's ancient capital, or Kanchanaburi, where the bridge over the Kwai River and the Allied cemeteries mark a tragic phase of World War II. If it is tropical beaches you long for, make for Pattaya, or Koh Samed with its powder-soft sands.

A resident at Khao Yai

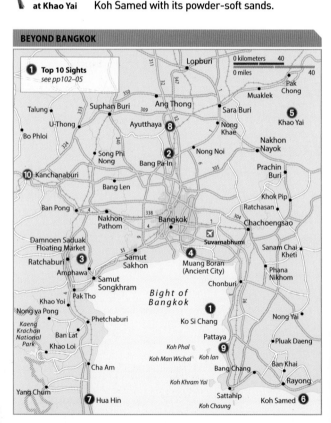

BEYOND BANGKOK

1. **Top 10 Sights**
   see pp102–05

1 Koh Si Chang

MAP U3 ▪ 62 miles (99 km) SE of Bangkok

Rarely visited by foreigners, this small, rocky island is located 5 miles (8 km) off the east Gulf coast. It has a selection of everything – secluded beaches with clear waters, a hilly interior ripe for exploring, and the remains of Rama V's palace, plus some reasonable accommodations. The most popular beach on the island is Tham Phang Beach.

2 Bang Pa-In

While visiting Ayutthaya, it is well worth stopping off at the nearby royal retreat of Bang Pa-In. Established by King Prasat Thong (r.1629–56) in the mid-17th century and expanded by Rama IV and Rama V (see p40), its exuberant buildings are an eclectic mix of Thai architecture, particularly in the Aisawan Thipphaya-at pavilion, and European influences, as seen in the Phra Thinang Warophat Phiman. The manicured lawns and tranquil lakes give the place a relaxed feel (see p36).

3 Damnoen Saduak Floating Market

Although this floating market is considered by some to be nothing more than a show put on for tourists, it is certainly the best example of its kind. The market gives an idea of how life in this region once revolved around small boats plying their trade on narrow canals. Arrive early (or even better, stay overnight) to avoid the crowds emerging from tour buses at around 10am, and you will be rewarded with images of smiling Thais in traditional clothes, *sampans* (flat-bottomed boats) piled high with appetizing fruits, and bowls of noodles served directly from floating kitchens (see pp26–7).

Damnoen Saduak Floating Market

4 Muang Boran (Ancient City)

MAP T2 ▪ 20 miles (33 km) from Bangkok on Sukhumvit Road, Bangpoo ▪ 02 709 1644 ▪ Open 9am–7pm daily ▪ Adm ▪ www.ancientsiam.com

Covering a huge 320 acres (130 ha) designed in the shape of Thailand, this cultural park contains reconstructions of some of the country's most famous temples and monuments. It may sound like a tacky theme park, but the site offers a visually impressive and informative experience. Visitors can explore the site by car, tram, or bicycle, and it is rarely crowded.

Lakeside pavilion at Muang Boran (Ancient City)

5 Khao Yai
MAP U1 ▪ 105 miles (170 km) NE of Bangkok

Thailand's first National Park, this mountainous, forested area is home to elephants, tigers, and gibbons, plus over 300 species of birds. There are several waterfalls and bat caves, as well as resorts and golf courses in the foothills outside the park's boundaries. Trekking and mountain biking tours are offered, as well as camping. Visitors should plan on spending the night here to fully appreciate this natural wonderland.

6 Koh Samed
MAP U3 ▪ 124 miles (200 km) SE of Bangkok

Easily the best beach escape from the capital, Koh Samed is an island with clear waters and fine sand, as well as a national park. Due to its popularity, accommodation rates have spiraled. By avoiding weekends and public holidays, it is possible to enjoy the idyllic surroundings without feeling like a sardine in a can.

Crystal-clear waters of Koh Samed

7 Hua Hin
MAP S3 ▪ 118 miles (190 km) SW of Bangkok

Thailand's oldest beach resort was popularized by the royal family when they had a summer palace built here in 1926. Though the 3-mile (5-km) beach is fine for a stroll or a pony ride, shade is limited, and the shallow bay can frustrate swimmers. Vestiges of the past remain in the train station and the squid piers along the front.

Ancient ruins at Ayutthaya

8 Ayutthaya

From 1350 to 1767, Ayutthaya ruled supreme as the capital of its own kingdom, only to be abandoned after being sacked by the Burmese (see p40). The Ayutthaya Historical Park features ancient ruins set in tranquil countryside. The main temples – Wat Ratchaburuna, Wat Mahathat, and Wat Sri Sanphet – can be covered in a day trip (see pp34–7).

9 Pattaya
MAP U3 ▪ 91 miles (147 km) SE of Bangkok

Pattaya is infamous for its go-go bars, discos, transvestite cabarets, and countless "bar beers" – open-sided bars with friendly hostesses. Yet the town has made an attempt to clean up its image, and there are now some family attractions, such as Pattaya Park Water Park, Mini Siam, Underwater World, and an Elephant Village. Watersports and golf are

---

THE DEATH RAILWAY

Between 1942–5, about 16,000 Allied prisoners of war and 100,000 Asians died during the construction of a railroad line from Thailand to Burma. The Japanese saw the line as crucial to their occupation of Southeast Asia. After the Japanese surrender, the British tore up the track. The rail link was never re-established.

also big here, and there are some excellent seafood restaurants and well-stocked shopping malls.

10 Kanchanaburi

MAP S2 ▪ 80 miles (130 km) W of Bangkok

At the western edge of the Central Plains, Kanchanaburi is a popular day trip from Bangkok. The main sights are the bridge over the Kwai River and the war cemeteries where thousands of allied soldiers who died in World War II during the construction of the "Death Railway" to Burma are buried. The Thailand-Burma Railway Center explains how the disastrous events unfolded. Kanchanaburi is also the jumping-off point for several natural sites, including the Erawan National Park, with its waterfalls.

Waterfalls near Kanchanaburi

▶ MORNING

Start the day relaxing on **Jomtien Beach**, a seemingly endless stretch of sand just south of Pattaya town center. Take a swim to cool down or if you are feeling energetic have a go at waterskiing, windsurfing, or parasailing. If you haven't been snacking all morning on seafood or fruit sold by wandering vendors on the beach, head for **Bruno's** near the north end of the beach for a steak or lobster lunch.

AFTERNOON

After lunch, head up to **Khao Phra Tamnak** from where there are excellent views of Pattaya Beach. Next, head north of town to the **Sanctuary of Truth**, a fabulous palace that blends influences from Khmer, Hindu, and Buddhist architecture. Finish the afternoon's sightseeing with a visit to **Mini Siam**, which features miniature models of some of the country's most famous buildings.

NIGHT

After a rest and shower in the hotel, head out for a taste of Pattaya's nightlife. Begin in any of the beachfront bar beers, where you can get a feel for the party mood of the town. For dinner, go to **PIC Kitchen** in Soi 5 and indulge in a delicious curry or freshly grilled seafood. Next, check out a Thai transvestite cabaret at **Tiffany's**. After the show, decide whether to head for bed or make a deeper exploration of Pattaya's pulsating nightlife.

See map on p102 ←

Streetsmart

Preparing and selling boat noodles
at a floating market in Bangkok

Getting To and Around Bangkok

Arriving by Air

Unless entering Thailand via a land crossing from Malaysia, Cambodia, or Laos, most travelers to Bangkok arrive by air. The city's **Suvarnabhumi** International Airport (BKK) is served by over 80 airlines with direct flights from most of the world's major cities. International and domestic flights all operate from the same terminal, with arrivals on Level 2 and departures on Level 4. The airport is around 16 miles (25 km) east of Bangkok. The old international airport, **Don Muang** International Airport (DMK), 16 miles (25 km) north of Bangkok, now serves as a hub for domestic and international low-cost airlines such as Nok Air, Thai Smile, Air Asia, and Thai Lion. Thai Airways has an extensive network, and budget airlines such as Air Asia operate flights within Thailand and to destinations in Southeast Asia and beyond.

The Suvarnabhumi Airport Rail Link (SARL) leaves from the basement of the airport terminal and provides transfers into the city for minimal costs. The SARL also connects with Bangkok's two MRT (mass rapid transit) systems – the Skytrain and the subway.

Arriving by Train

It is possible to reach Bangkok from Singapore and Malaysia by train. All trains terminate at **Hua Lampong Station.**

Arriving by Bus

Thailand fits well into overland itineraries that include visits to neighboring countries. Buses from Malaysia terminate at the **Southern Bus Terminal**, while those from Cambodia and Laos arrive at the **Northern Bus Terminal** at Mochit.

Traveling by Skytrain

Bangkok's first and most useful mass rapid transit system is the **Skytrain**, an elevated railway with two lines. The Sukhumvit Line runs from Chatuchak Weekend Market, through the downtown shopping area at Rama I and Ploenchit roads, along Sukhumvit Road to Soi Thonglor, and into the eastern suburbs. The Silom Line runs from the National Stadium (near Jim Thompson House), through the downtown Silom area, to Saphan Taksin (good for accessing river boats), and over the river into Thonburi. The two lines intersect at Siam Square. The Skytrain connects to the high-speed rail link to Suvarnabhumi Airport at Phaya Thai Station.

The system gets very busy during rush hours (7–9am and 5–7pm). To avoid the lines at the ticket vending machines, go to the manned ticket counters and buy a one-day pass for B140 (unlimited trips) or a Rabbit Card (stored-value card) for B300. The last train is at midnight.

Traveling by MRT

The **MRT** subway system covers a 12-mile (20-km) loop from Hua Lampong Station, passing through Silom and Sukhumvit downtown areas, and continuing to Chatuchak Weekend Market and into Bangkok's northern suburbs. Extension work is underway, and the route will continue from Hua Lampong into the Old City and Chinatown.

The MRT intersects with the Skytrain at four stations, but transferring between systems requires buying a new ticket. The system connects with the Suvarnabhumi Airport Rail Link at Makkasan Station.

The MRT offers day passes and stored-value cards. Like the Skytrain, the MRT gets very busy during rush hours, and it's best to plan trips outside those times if possible. The last train is at midnight.

Traveling by Bus

BMTA runs an extensive bus network with very cheap fares. Most routes operate 4am–10pm, with a few providing a 24-hour service. Buses can get stuck in heavy traffic, so an air-conditioned bus is a good option.

Traveling by Taxi

Metered taxis are easy to find and relatively cheap, with a flag fare of B35 for the first 0.6 miles (1 km) and B5.5 for every 0.6 mile (1 km) after that.

The meter also calculates time, charging for slow-moving traffic. A short journey costs about B60. Insist on using the meter, since it is cheaper than negotiating a fare.

App-based taxi services such as **All Thai Taxi** (which uses standard Thai taxis) and **Uber** (choice of vehicle) operate in Bangkok.

Traveling by Tuk-Tuk

A ride in a tuk-tuk is an essential part of the Thai experience, and it can be exciting weaving through traffic in these open-sided three-wheelers. However, they are noisy and unprotected from pollution. Fares must be negotiated before you start.

Traveling by Motorbike Taxi

Motorbike taxi riders who wait on the corners of important side roads are useful for routes not covered by other modes of transport. Fares are negotiable, starting at B20 for a short trip. They are fast and can squeeze through traffic jams, but can be dangerous, so do hang on tight.

Traveling on Foot

The key to a pleasant walk in Bangkok is to avoid major thoroughfares and walk in the quiet *sois* (lanes) that run parallel to the main roads. Use a good street map to plot your route via the *sois*. Dedicated walkers should try to find a copy of Ken Barrett's excellent *22 Walks in Bangkok*, or join a guided walking tour.

Traveling by Car

Without detailed road knowledge, city driving can be very frustrating. Car rental companies such as **Hertz** and **Budget** also offer drivers.

Traveling by Bicycle

Bike-shares and rentals exist here, and the Old City has dedicated bike lanes, but it's best to start with a cycling tour. Try **Follow Me**, **Pun Pun Bike Share**, or **Spice Roads**.

Traveling by Boat

Chao Phraya and **Khlong Saen Saeb** express boat services *(see p21)* are good for sightseeing and transportation, especially to go from Downtown to the Old City until the new MRT stations open. Hotels on the Thonburi side offer free shuttles. Chartering a longtail boat is an option.

Buying tickets

Buy a stored-value card or day pass at a manned ticket office to avoid lines at Skytrain and MRT vending machines. You can buy train tickets in advance at Hua Lampong Station or from travel agents.

DIRECTORY

ARRIVING BY AIR

Don Muang
W donmuangairport
online.com

Suvarnabhumi
W suvarnabhumiairport.
com

ARRIVING BY TRAIN

Hua Lampong Station
MAP F6 ∎ Rama IV Rd
C 02 225 6964

ARRIVING BY BUS

Northern Bus Terminal
MAP T5 ∎
Phahonyothin Rd
C 02 272 0299

Southern Bus Terminal
MAP S5 ∎ Borommarat
Chonnani Rd
C 02 435 1199

TRAVELING BY SKYTRAIN

Skytrain
W bts.co.th

TRAVELING BY MRT

MRT
W bangkokmetro.co.th

TRAVELING BY BUS

BMTA
W bmta.co.th

TRAVELING BY TAXI

All Thai Taxi
W allthaitaxi.com

Uber
W uber.com

TRAVELING BY CAR

Budget
W budget.co.th

Hertz
W hertzthailand.com

TRAVELING BY BICYCLE

Follow Me
W followmebiketour.
com

Pun Pun Bike Share
W punpunbikeshare.
com

Spice Roads
W spiceroads.com

BOAT

Chao Phraya
W chaophrayaexpress
boat.com

Khlong Saen Saeb
W khlongsaensaep.com

Practical Information

Passports and Visas

All visitors to Thailand must be in possession of a passport valid for at least six months from the date of entry. People from most Western countries are given a 30-day tourist visa on arrival at the airport. For longer visits, apply at the nearest Thai embassy for a 60-day visa, which must be used within three months of issue. Non-immigrant 90-day visas are available if there is a good reason for an extended stay, such as education or business. For a fee, 30- and 60-day visas can be extended by 30 days at the **Immigration Office**. If you overstay your visa, there is a B500 fine per day. These regulations are subject to change, so check the **Thai Ministry of Foreign Affairs** website.

Numerous countries, including **Australia**, the **UK**, and the **US**, have consular representation in the city.

Customs Regulations

The duty-free allowance for passengers arriving in Thailand is 200 cigarettes or 9 oz (250 g) of tobacco and a liter of wines or spirits. E-cigarettes and pornography are banned. Inspection of incoming tourists is cursory at best.

Travel Safety Advice

Get up-to-date travel safety information from the **UK Foreign and Commonwealth Office**, the **US State Department**, and the **Australian Department of Foreign Affairs and Trade**.

Travel Insurance

Travel insurance is strongly recommended, particularly as healthcare can be costly. Be sure to double check that your policy covers Thailand, along with theft and accidental loss, before traveling.

Health

Healthcare is good and affordable, and the country is a popular medical tourism destination. **Bumrungrad Hospital** and **Bangkok Nursing Home (BNH) Hospital** are good for serious issues and surgery. In an emergency, call the **Medical Hotline**. For minor ailments, local clinics are also hygienic and reliable, and staff speak essential English. Pharmacies are generally well stocked. Prescriptions are not necessary for antibiotics. Dental care at places like the **Dental Hospital** is inexpensive and good. No vaccinations are required for entering the country. Tropical diseases such as malaria don't exist here, but sexually transmitted diseases are a problem so protection is suggested.

Personal Security

Bangkok is fairly safe, but it is wise to store cash in your hotel safe. Avoid wearing expensive jewelry in public and watch out for pickpockets in crowded areas and ensure bags are theft-proof. Violent incidents are rare and usually linked to too much alcohol, as are assaults on women. Contact the **Tourist Police** if you have a problem. It is wise to avoid political demonstrations here.

Banking

Thailand's currency is the *baht* (B), divided into 100 *satang*. There are B1, B2, B5, and B10 coins; notes are available for B20 (green), B50 (blue), B100 (red), B500 (purple), and B1,000 (brown).

Most banks, including **Bangkok Bank** and **Thai Military Bank**, are open 8:30am–3:30pm Monday–Friday, but branches in airports and department stores often stay open later and on weekends. Big branches have a foreign-exchange counter, can arrange international transfers, and offer the best exchange rate.

ATMs can be found outside bank branches, mini-marts, and department stores. All offer an English-language option and accept major credit and debit cards, but a service charge is applied.

VISA and MasterCard credit and debit cards are accepted by major banks, travel agents, department stores, hotels, and most restaurants. American Express and Diners Club are not widely accepted.

Postal Services

Post office hours are normally 8:30am–4:30pm Monday–Friday and 9am–noon on Saturday. Letters to or from Europe or the US take at least a week to arrive. For important documents, use the Express Mail Service (EMS) or pay a fee to register the letter.

Media

Some guesthouses and many hotels offer satellite TV with English channels. There are also a few radio stations that broadcast in English, such as **Eazy FM** and **Radio Thailand**. Two English dailies, *Bangkok Post* and *The Nation*, carry news and listings. Copies of international papers such as the UK's *The Times* and *USA Today* are sold in some bookshops, though prices for these are steep.

Opening Hours

Most government offices are open 8:30am–4:30pm on weekdays, but many close for lunch. Tourist attractions tend to open 9am–5pm daily. Department stores open daily at 10am and close at 9 or 10pm. On public holidays, government offices, post offices, and banks are closed, but most shops, bars and restaurants remain open.

Time Difference

Thailand is seven hours ahead of Greenwich Mean Time, 12 hours ahead of US Eastern Standard Time, and three hours behind Australian Eastern Standard Time.

Electrical Appliances

The electric current in Thailand is 220 volts AC, 50 Hz, and most plug sockets are of the two-pin variety. Adaptors are readily available in department stores.

Weather

The best time to visit is November–February, with clear skies and cooler temperatures, generally around 80° F (26.5° C). However, hotel rates tend to be higher, and tourist attractions more crowded. The hot season (March–May) is fine for a beach holiday but not for sightseeing. The rainy season (June–October) can be pleasant, and storms usually blow over quickly.

The tropical monsoon climate means that spring is hot, followed by summer rains. Loose, breathable clothes are best, and layering a long-sleeved top over a T-shirt also provides sun protection. Bangkokians see short pants as beachwear, but visitors are given latitude, except in temples. During the rainy season umbrella vendors are everywhere.

DIRECTORY

PASSPORTS AND VISAS

Australian Embassy
🔲 thailand.embassy.gov. au

Immigration Office
🔲 bangkok.immigration. go.th

Thai Ministry of Foreign Affairs
🔲 mfa.go.th

UK Embassy
🔲 gov.uk/government/ world/organisations/ british-embassy-bangkok

US Embassy
🔲 th.usembassy.gov

TRAVEL SAFETY ADVICE

Australian Department of Foreign Affairs and Trade
🔲 dfat.gov.au
🔲 smartraveller.gov.au

UK Foreign and Commonwealth Office
🔲 gov.uk/foreign-travel-advice

US Department of State
🔲 travel.state.gov

HEALTH

BNH Hospital
🔲 bnhhospital.com

Bumrungrad Hospital
🔲 bumrungrad.com

Dental Hospital
🔲 dentalhospital bangkok.com

Medical Hotline
📞 1669

PERSONAL SECURITY

Tourist Police
📞 1155
🔲 thailand touristpolice. com

BANKING

Bangkok Bank
📞 1333, +66 (0) 2645 5555 (from abroad)
🔲 bangkokbank.com

Thai Military Bank
📞 1558, +662 299 1558 (from abroad)
🔲 tmbbank.com

MEDIA

Bangkok Post
🔲 bangkokpost.com

Eazy FM
🔲 eazyfm.becteroradio. com

Radio Thailand
🔲 hsk9.org

The Nation
🔲 nationmultimedia. com

Travelers with Disabilities

Thailand has made progress in improving wheelchair accessibility, with many hotels and departments stores providing ramps and elevators. Sidewalks are not wheelchair-friendly. However, what the city lacks in infrastructure for the disabled is made up by the helpful nature of the people. Specialized tour agencies cater to those with specific needs. **Accessible Thailand** can provide more information.

Sources of Information

The **Tourism Authority of Thailand**, the official government tourist board, has offices worldwide and its headquarters in Bangkok. Its website provides comprehensive coverage of destinations and events, and maps and brochures are available from its office. The **Bangkok Tourism Division** is also a useful source of information and has booths in many of the city's tourist areas.

Some of the best Bangkok travel tips come from two monthly magazines, *Bangkok 101* and *The Big Chili*, which are sold in bookstores (although both have good websites). Mainly directed toward expats, they offer the latest in dining, nightlife, and general exploring, and they are much more reliable than the many blogs and click-driven websites. *BK* magazine, distributed free in hotels, offers useful listings.

Trips and Tours

Planning a journey in a crowded, unfamiliar city can be difficult, so many people opt for a guided tour. While such tours may be enjoyable and informative, they are also expensive and preclude encounters with local people that can lead to stimulating cultural exchanges. We recommend self-guiding for the major sites (see Exploring Bangkok, pp6–7) and using tours focused on special interests, such as culinary tours, tours organized by art museums, or activities requiring special equipment, such as cycling.

Shopping

Bangkok is a shopper's paradise and runs the gamut from the glitziest malls to sidewalk vendors. The massive and ultra-modern shopping malls in Siam Square and Sukhumvit are like small cities, containing department stores, food courts, bowling alleys, designer boutiques, and skating rinks. Shopping in markets and at street stalls combines the opportunity to pick up bargains with cultural interaction. The best markets for textiles or ready-made clothes are Chatuchak (see pp28–9), Phahurat (see p77), and Pratunam (see p60), while street stalls in Khao San Road, Patpong, and Sukhumvit Road are good for souvenirs.

Prices are fixed in shopping malls and boutiques, but bargaining is expected in markets and at street stalls, where vendors quote a price that may be up to double the object's value. Start by offering a figure less than what you are prepared to pay and gradually increase the offer until a deal is struck. Keep smiling! If all else fails, walking away may persuade a vendor to drop the price.

Thai handicrafts make great souvenirs and gifts. These are widely available in Bangkok at markets such as Chatuchak. Items on offer include clothes and bags made of silk and cotton, baskets, ceramics, lacquerware, wall hangings, and woodcarvings. Gold in Thailand is 24 karat and sold by weight, its value varying according to the world market. Colored gems such as rubies and sapphires are very alluring, but unless you are an expert, confine any purchases to high-end shops, such as those in **Peninsula Plaza**, since inferior gems and fakes abound. Custom-tailored clothing is also of interest, but only the best shops, like **Tailor on Ten**, use fabrics of high quality, and several fittings are required for a good result. Antiques are also worth considering, but similar to newly cast Buddha images, they require a special export permit from the Department of Fine Arts. The export of antique Buddhas is forbidden.

Thais produce excellent copies of anything from branded watches to designer clothes. Western countries' customs take fakes seriously, and confiscation – or even prosecution – is possible.

Where to Eat

While in Bangkok, you can eat in fancy restaurants, at street stalls, and everywhere in between. While only a few restaurants are expensive, some of Bangkok's best food can be found at street stalls, so be adventurous and try everything. Choose street food in places off the main roads, where it's cooler and quieter. Don't miss the food courts found in most shopping malls – the prices are only slightly above street-food prices, and the air-conditioning makes things more comfortable. Food courts use a coupon system – you pay at a central kiosk rather than paying the vendors.

Thais love children, and even if kids' menus are rare, taking children along for a meal makes everyone happy.

The concept of tipping, once alien to Thais, has been happily embraced by restaurant staff. This is especially true for tourist areas. The 10–15 percent rule followed in the West does not apply in Bangkok. Leave whatever you think the staff deserve; every *baht* will be appreciated. High-end restaurants often add a service charge; if so, no tip is necessary.

Where to Stay

In Bangkok, five-star accommodation can cost as little as a mid-range hotel in Europe or the US. For your money, you can expect a large room with a decent view, luxurious furnishings and decor,

plenty of on-site bars and restaurants and attentive service (see pp114–15).

Mid-range hotels offer all the basic comforts, like air-conditioned rooms, bathrooms with hot water, and TVs, though without the luxurious touches and elegance of top-end hotels. Within this price range, it is worth checking out the rapidly growing number of boutique hotels that offer a more personal touch and unique character, often missing even in top-end hotels (see pp115–16).

Bangkok attracts a stream of budget tourists, mostly to Khao San Road, the "backpackers' ghetto." A typical cheap room will be small, often without windows, with a bed, a fan, paper-thin walls, and shared bathrooms. Khao San Road is great for dining and nightlife, but nearby areas are worth exploring for quieter accommodations (see p117). **Agoda** is a useful booking resource. **Airbnb**, the online peer-to-peer accommodation service, also operates in Bangkok and offers good opportunities to meet with and get to know locals.

Rates and Booking

It is a good idea to book your hotel room well in advance of your visit, especially if the hotel in question is highly rated, and even more so during the high season (Nov–Feb) or major festivals. Internet booking services are useful, but be sure to check change and cancellation policies before booking. Some

hotels offer good rates on their own websites. If using Airbnb, double-check the location of the property, since many of the listings are far from the center of the city.

Hotel rates hit a peak during the cool season (Nov–Feb), when many establishments operate at full occupancy. For the rest of the year, it is worth asking about discounts, especially if you plan to stay several nights. Some budget hotels and guesthouses also offer competitive monthly rates.

DIRECTORY

TRAVELERS WITH DISABILITIES

Accessible Thailand
🌐 accessiblethailand.com

SOURCES OF INFORMATION

Bangkok Tourism Division
MAP C2 ■ 17/1 Phra Athit Road
📞 02 225 7612–4
🌐 bangkoktourist.com

Tourism Authority of Thailand
Off MAP R2 ■ 1600 Petchaburi Road
📞 1672 (toll-free)
🌐 tourismthailand.org

SHOPPING

Tailor on Ten
MAP T6 ■ Sukhumvit Soi 8
📞 (084) 877 1543

Peninsula Plaza
MAP Q3 ■ 153 Ratchadamri Road
📞 02 253 9791

ACCOMMODATION

Agoda
🌐 agoda.com

Airbnb
🌐 airbnb.com

Places to Stay

PRICE CATEGORIES
For a standard, double room per night (with breakfast
if included), taxes and extra charges.

B under B1,500   **BB** B1,500–4,000   **BBB** over B4,000

Luxury Hotels

Anantara Bangkok Riverside Resort and Spa

MAP S6 ▪ 257 Charoen Nakhon Road, Thonburi ▪ 02 476 0022 ▪ www.anantara.com ▪ BBB
Built on prime property on the west bank of the Chao Phraya River, this huge complex has a lovely spa, fine gardens, many restaurants, and an exotic pool. Each room has a private balcony.

Anantara Siam

MAP Q3 ▪ 55 Ratchadamri Road ▪ 02 126 8866 ▪ www.anantara.com ▪ BBB
Luxurious rooms, impeccable service, and a number of fine-dining restaurants make this one of Bangkok's best hotels. It is in an excellent location, with views over the green expanse of the Royal Bangkok Sports Club.

COMO Metropolitan Bangkok

MAP Q5 ▪ 27 South Sathorn Road ▪ 02 625 3333 ▪ www.comohotels.com ▪ BBB
Bangkok's trendiest hotel features a minimalist look and silk furnishings. Its two great restaurants, Nahm and Glow, and the members-only Met Bar attract the city's top design gurus.

Conrad Hotel

MAP R3 ▪ All Seasons Place, Withayu Road ▪ 02 690 9999 ▪ www.conradhotels.com ▪ BBB
Designed in contemporary Thai style, making lavish use of silk and wood, Conrad Hotel has lovely views over Lumphini Park (see p86). It has a central location, and its restaurants and bars are among the best in town.

Grand Hyatt Erawan Bangkok

MAP Q3 ▪ 494 Ratchadamri Road ▪ 02 254 1234 ▪ www.bangkok.hyatt.com ▪ BBB
A grandiose entrance leads to guest rooms with large windows, marble baths, and trendy fittings. The afternoon tea in the Garden Lounge is a delight.

Mandarin Oriental Hotel

MAP M5 ▪ 48 Oriental Avenue ▪ 02 659 9000 ▪ www.mandarinoriental.com/bangkok ▪ BBB
The historic Oriental (see p85) has often been voted the world's best hotel for its superb facilities, exceptional views, and personalized service.

The Peninsula Hotel

MAP L5 ▪ 333 Charoen Nakhon Road ▪ 02 020 2888 ▪ www.bangkok.peninsula.com ▪ BBB
The Peninsula has won several awards for its wave-shaped design and spacious guest rooms with fabulous views of the Chao Phraya River and the city. It has a three-tiered swimming pool, a gorgeous spa and restaurants serving Thai, and Cantonese cuisine.

Royal Orchid Sheraton

MAP M4 ▪ 2 Captain Bush Lane ▪ 02 266 0123 ▪ www.starwoodhotels.com/sheraton/bangkok ▪ BBB
This 28-story hotel has pools and tennis courts, a fitness center and spa, restaurants serving royal Thai and Italian cuisine, and a relaxed riverside bar.

Shangri-La Hotel

MAP M6 ▪ 89 Soi Wat Suan Phlu, Charoen Krung Road ▪ 02 236 7777 ▪ www.shangri-la.com ▪ BBB
With 800 rooms, the riverside Shangri-La is one of Bangkok's biggest luxury hotels. It has several restaurants and bars; the excellent Chi, The Spa (see p46); a fitness center, pools, and tennis courts.

Siam Kempinski Hotel

MAP P2 ▪ 991/9 Rama I Road ▪ 02 162 9000 ▪ www.kempinski.com/bangkok ▪ BBB
An Art Deco-inspired resort hotel in the heart of the city, the beautiful Siam Kempinski is set around a landscaped garden and has three pools. It also has a spa and an excellent contemporary Thai restaurant.

Sukhothai Hotel

MAP Q5 ▪ 13/3 South Sathorn Road ▪ 02 344 8888 ▪ www.sukhothai. com ▪ BBB

The Sukhothai Hotel combines traditional Thai architecture with modern conveniences. Surrounded by lush gardens and pools, the hotel has luxurious rooms, three excellent restaurants, and a pool-terrace café.

W Hotel

MAP P6 ▪ 106 North Sathorn Road ▪ 02 344 4000 ▪ www.starwood hotels.com ▪ BBB

Chic and sleek, with many imaginative twists, this oasis of modern luxury also includes The House on Sathorn, a colonial mansion that once housed the Russian Embassy, now a sumptuous restaurant and bar. Their Woo Bar is a Bangkok hot spot.

Business Hotels

Dusit Thani Hotel

MAP Q5 ▪ 946 Rama IV Road ▪ 02 236 9999 ▪ www.dusit.com ▪ BBB

One of Bangkok's biggest and oldest hotels, the Dusit Thani has a perfect location right opposite serene Lumphini Park (see p86). Its rooms are lavishly decorated with teak furnishings and lovely silk trimmings.

InterContinental Hotel

MAP R3 ▪ 973 Ploenchit Road ▪ 02 656 0444 ▪ www.intercontinental. com ▪ BBB

Towering above Chitlom's business district, this 37-story hotel is perfect for business travelers and shoppers, with the Skytrain

right at its doorstep. Huge rooms offer great views from the double-glazed, soundproofed windows.

Lebua at State Tower

MAP N5 ▪ 1055 Silom Road ▪ 02 624 9999 ▪ www.lebua.com ▪ BBB

This distinctive skyscraper with its golden dome is one of Bangkok's icons. It is also home to Breeze (see p91) and Sirocco, two of the city's top dining venues, as well as the stunning Sky Bar (see p92).

Majestic Grande Sukhumvit

MAP T6 ▪ 12 Sukhumvit Soi 2 ▪ 02 262 2999 ▪ www.majesticgrande. com ▪ BBB

Conveniently located, this opulent hotel offers an excellent range of facilities for business guests, including generous desk space in the rooms and a translation service in the business center.

Sheraton Grande Sukhumvit

MAP T6 ▪ 250 Sukhumvit Road ▪ 02 649 8888 ▪ www.sheratongrande-sukhumvit.com ▪ BBB

Among Bangkok's best business hotels, the Sheraton Grande offers modern elegance with state-of-the-art facilities. Its business center is open 24 hours, and a footbridge connects the hotel to the Asoke Skytrain station.

Westin Grande Sukhumvit

MAP T6 ▪ 259 Sukhumvit Road ▪ 02 207 8000 ▪ www.westin.com/ bangkok ▪ BBB

The rooms are designed with executive travelers in

mind, complete with soft beds and flat-screen TVs. The Vareena Spa and the Zest Bar and Terrace have panoramic views.

Mid-Range Hotels

Aloft Hotel Bangkok

MAP T6 ▪ 35 Sukhumvit Soi 11 ▪ 02 207 7000 ▪ www.aloftbangkok-sukhumvit11.com ▪ BB

Sheraton's mid-range chain provides trendy decor, large rooms, and efficient service. Levels (see p93), one of the city's hottest nightspots, is downstairs. Soi 11 has many cafés and pubs.

Chillax Resort

MAP C2 ▪ 274 Samsen Road Soi 2 ▪ 02 629 4400 ▪ www.chillaxresort.com ▪ BB

This high-rise hotel has a rooftop infinity pool with incredible views over the city and the river. Each room has a Jacuzzi, good for unwinding after a long day's sightseeing.

Navalai River Resort

MAP C2 ▪ 45 Phra Athit Road ▪ 02 280 9955 ▪ www.navalai.com ▪ BB

Located on hip Phra Athit Road, near the Grand Palace, the Navalai has balconied rooms overlooking the Chao Phraya and a rooftop pool. There is also a riverside restaurant.

New Siam Riverside

MAP B2 ▪ 21 Phra Athit Road ▪ 02 629 3535 ▪ www.newsiam.net ▪ BB

This clean and quiet inn offers the best budget rooms on the river in the lively Phra Athit area, near Khao San Road.

Rembrandt Hotel

MAP T6 ■ 19 Sukhumvit Soi 18 ■ 02 261 7100 ■ www.rembrandtbkk.com ■ BB

In a quiet *soi* off the main Sukhumvit Road, near Soi Asok, the Rembrandt offers value well beyond its price and immaculate rooms, as well as the best Indian and Mexican restaurants in the city.

The Rose Hotel

MAP P5 ■ 118 Surawong Road ■ 02 266 8268 ■ www.rosehotelbkk.com ■ BB

Close to much of the Silom area's shopping and nightlife, the Rose offers comfortable, quiet rooms in contemporary Asian style. It has a swimming pool, an excellent restaurant, a gym, and a sauna.

Wall Street Inn

MAP P5 ■ 37/20–24 Surawong Road ■ 02 233 4144 ■ www.wallstreet innhotel.com ■ BB

The smartly furnished rooms in this hotel come with comfortable beds, satellite TV, and bath tubs. There is also a business center, a coffee shop, and a massage parlor offering traditional massage and foot reflexology.

Boutique Hotels

AriyasomVilla Boutique Hotel

MAP T6 ■ 65 Sukhumvit Soi 1 ■ 02 254 8880 ■ www.ariyasom.com ■ BB

This 1940s mansion is a serene urban oasis close to the Saen Saeb canal and downtown shopping areas. There's a lovely garden and pool, and great vegetarian food.

Luxx Hotel

MAP N5 ■ 6/11 Decho Rd ■ 02 635 8800 ■ www.staywithluxx.com ■ BB

The minimalist appearance of the suites and compact rooms at this hotel will appeal to the young, hip, and trendy; and the location, just a few steps from the shops and nightlife of Silom Road, could not be better.

Praya Palazzo

MAP B2 ■ 757/1 Somdet Phra Pin Klao, Soi 2 ■ 02 883 2998 ■ www.praya palazzo.com ■ BB

With a riverfront location on the Thonburi side, this restored Italianate mansion is beautifully decorated and serves excellent Thai and Western food.

Shanghai Mansion

MAP L3 ■ 479–81 Yaowarat Road ■ 02 221 2121 ■ www.shanghai mansion.com ■ BB

In the heart of Chinatown, this chic and unusual hotel has just over 50 smallish rooms fitted with four-poster beds and painted in vibrant colors. Some are window-less. There is a restaurant, massage/spa facilities, and a shuttle tuk-tuk service for guests.

Siam Heritage

MAP P5 ■ 115/1 Surawong Road ■ 02 353 6166 ■ www.thesiam heritage.com ■ BB

The rooms of this hotel are decorated in Northern and Central Thai style, with polished wood floors and antique furnishings. Services include a spa, a business center, and a terrace restaurant.

Chakrabongse Villas

MAP B5 ■ 396 Maharaj Road ■ 02 222 1290 ■ www.thaivillas.com ■ BBB

Located on the Chao Phraya River, near Wat Pho and with amazing views of Wat Arun, this stunning hotel comprises seven rooms and suites set in lush tropical gardens, with a riverside dining terrace.

The Siam

MAP S5 ■ 3/2 Thanon Khao, behind Vachira Hospital ■ 02 206 9999 ■ www.thesiamhotel.com ■ BBB

Bangkok's top-rated small hotel, located in the quiet Dusit area, has 39 sumptuously decorated suites and villas with antique furniture and lovely views of the river.

Budget

A-One Inn

MAP P2 ■ 25/13 Soi Kasemsan 1, Rama I Road ■ 02 215 3029 ■ www.aoneinn.com ■ B

Tucked just around the corner from Siam Square, the shoppers' paradise, this upscale guesthouse has basic but clean rooms. The staff are friendly, there is Internet access, and it is only a few steps from the National Stadium BTS station.

Jim's Lodge

MAP R3 ■ 25/7 Soi Ruamrudee, Ploenchit Road ■ 02 255 3100 ■ www.jimslodge.com ■ B

Located near several major embassies and shopping malls, Jim's Lodge offers good-sized, well-equipped standard and superior rooms, as well as suites. Service is very efficient, and the lodge's other amenities include a restaurant.

Riverview Guesthouse

MAP E6 ▪ 768 Songwat Road ▪ 02 235 8501 ▪ www.riverviewbkk. com ▪ B

Located in a backstreet beside the San Jao Sien Khong temple in Chinatown, this family-run guesthouse has refurbished rooms and good views of the Chao Phraya River from the upper floors. There is a great rooftop bar and restaurant.

Silom Village Inn

MAP N5 ▪ 286 Silom Road ▪ 02 635 6810 ▪ www.silomvillage.co.th/ hotel_silom.php ▪ B

Built to recreate the atmosphere of a traditional Thai village in Bangkok's most famous nightlife district, this small hotel offers superior and deluxe rooms, as well as suites at affordable rates. The hotel also hosts nightly cultural shows at the adjoining entertainment hall.

Suk 11

MAP T6 ▪ 1/33 Sukhumvit Soi 11 ▪ 02 253 5927 ▪ www.suk11.com ▪ B

Representing one of the city's best budget deals for its great location and quirky design, Suk 11 is one of Bangkok's most popular guesthouses. The rooms are small and basic, some with a shared toilet and hot shower, but all come with air-conditioning.

New Siam 2

MAP B2 ▪ 50 Trok Rong Mai, Phra Athit Road ▪ 02 282 2795 ▪ www.new siam.net ▪ BB

This modern budget hotel offers peace and privacy near the Grand Palace. Rooms are well equipped with in-room safes and private bathrooms, while air-conditioning costs extra. There is a small swimming pool.

Beyond Bangkok

Hilton Hua Hin Resort & Spa

MAP S3 ▪ 33 Soi Nares Damri, Hua Hin ▪ 032 538 999 ▪ www3.hilton. com ▪ BB

There may be newer and more spectacular hotels in Hua Hin, but the Hilton is within walking distance of old Hua Hin and the Night Market. It also fronts onto a beautiful beach, and its top-floor restaurant is one of the best in town.

Kantary Hotel

MAP T1 ▪ 168 Moo 1, Rojana Road, Ayutthaya ▪ 035 337 177 ▪ www. kantarycollection.com ▪ BB

This is the best choice for an overnight's stay in Ayutthaya. A great-value stylish hotel with ideal studios for families, the place also offers good tours of the historical sights.

Bangkok Tree House

MAP T6 ▪ 60 Moo 1, Petch Cha Heung Road, Bang Namphueng ▪ 08 2995 1150 ▪ www. bangkoktreehouse.com ▪ BBB

A boutique eco-resort located in Bang Krajao,

Bangkok's green lung (see p53), the Tree House is accessible only by boat or on foot. So close yet so different from the metropolis, it offers organic food and free bicycles – ideal for exploring this rural area.

Dheva Mantra Resort & Spa

MAP S2 ▪ Moo 3, Thamakham Road, Kanchanaburi ▪ 034 615 999 ▪ www.dheva mantra.com ▪ BBB

The sumptuous rooms here are set in an elegant colonial-style building and surrounded by huge gardens. Although it is a bit out of town, there are some great views over the river and mountains. There's also an excellent spa.

Novotel Suvarnabhumi Airport Hotel

MAP T2 ▪ Moo 1, Nongprue, Bang Phli, Samut Prakarn ▪ 02 131 1111 ▪ www. novotel. com ▪ BBB

If an airport hotel is needed, this is by far the best. The rooms are very elegant, and there is an excellent spa. Enjoy a relaxing atmosphere, and good food at any of the five restaurants and bars situated just off the atrium lobby.

Sugar Hut

MAP U3 ▪ 391/18 Moo 10, Thabpraya Road, Pattaya ▪ 038 251 686 ▪ www. sugar-hut.com ▪ BBB

Stay here for elegant Thai-style villas beyond the busy part of town, with superb gardens, three pools, and great Thai food.

For a key to hotel price categories see p114

Index

Acknowledgments

Author

Ron Emmons is a Thailand-based British writer and photographer whose work has appeared in a wide variety of international magazines and guidebooks, including the DK Eyewitness Travel Guide to Malaysia and Singapore.

Additional contributor
Peter Holmshaw

Publishing Director Georgina Dee

Publisher Vivien Antwi

Design Director Phil Ormerod

Editorial Sophie Adam, Ankita Awasthi Tröger, Avanika, Michelle Crane, Rachel Fox, Lucy Richards, Sally Schafer, Sands Publishing Solutions

Design Tessa Bindloss, Sunita Gahir, Bharti Karakoti, Rahul Kumar

Cover Design Richard Czapnik

Commissioned Photography David Henley, Alex Robinson, Rough Guides / Martin Richardson

Picture Research Susie Peachey, Ellen Root, Lucy Sienkowska, Oran Tarjan

Cartography Jasneet Kaur, Zafar ul Islam Khan, Suresh Kumar, James Macdonald, Reetu Pandey

DTP Jason Little

Production Poppy Werder-Harris

Factchecker Paul Gray

Proofreader Leena Lane

Indexer Helen Peters

Gaggan: 59bl.

Getty Images: AFP / Stan Honda 41tr, / Pornchai Kittiwongsakul 52clb; AWL / Gavin Hellier 89t; Paula Bronstein 41cl; Greg Elms 28-9; Kangheewan 70b; LightRocket / David Longstreath 64b; LightRocket / John S Lander 53cr; Lonely Planet Images / Frank Carter 78t; Moment / thebang 104clb; Seng Chye Teo 94ca; Universal History Archive 40cb.

Grand Hyatt Erawan Bangkok: 47cr.

Hard Rock Café Bangkok: 93tl.

The Jim Thompson House: Dorling Kindersley / Alex Robinson 30cla, 30br, 31crb.

Maggie Choo's: 56b, 93cr.

Mandarin Oriental, Bangkok: 46tr, 51cr, 58t.

The Museum of Floral Culture: 19NOVphotography 53tl.

National Museum, Bangkok: Dorling Kindersley / Alex Robinson 17bl, 68tl.

Robert Harding Picture Library: Kay Maeritz 16cla; Marco Simoni 19bl; Luca Tettoni 11cr, 12cla, 84cla.

Shangri-La Hotel Bangkok: 46bl.

The Sukhothai Bangkok: 99cb.

Tower Club at lebua: 91cra.

Cover
Front and spine: **Getty Images:** Marcus Mok.
Back: **Dreamstime.com:** John6863373.

Pull Out Map Cover
Getty Images: Marcus Mok.

All other images © Dorling Kindersley
For further information see:
www.dkimages.com

Penguin
Random
House

Printed and bound in China

First published in Great Britain in 2008
by Dorling Kindersley Limited
80 Strand, London WC2R 0RL

Copyright 2008, 2017 © Dorling
Kindersley Limited

A Penguin Random House Company

17 18 19 20 10 9 8 7 6 5 4 3 2 1

Reprinted with revisions 2010, 2012, 2014, 2017

ISBN 978 0 2412 7872 7

MIX
Paper from
responsible sources
FSC™ C018179

As a guide to abbreviations in visitor information blocks: **Adm** *= admission charge;* **DA** *= disabled access;* **D** *= dinner;* **L** *= lunch.*

Phrase Book

Thai is a tonal language and regarded by most linguists as head of a distinct language group, though it incorporates many Sanskrit words from ancient India, and some of modern English ones, too. There are five tones: mid, high, low, rising, and falling. The particular tone, or pitch, at which each syllable is pronounced determines its meaning. For instance "mâi" (falling tone) means "not," but "măi" (rising tone) is "silk." In the second column of this phrase book is a phonetic transliteration of the Thai script for English speakers, including guidance for tones in the form of accents. In polite speech, Thai men add **"krúp"** at the end of each sentence; women add **"kà"** at the end of questions and **"kǎ"** at the end of statements

Guidelines for Pronunciation

When reading the phonetics, pronounce syllables as if they form English words. For instance:

a	as in "ago"
e	as in "hen"
i	as in "thin"
o	as in "on"
u	as in "gun"
ah	as in "rather"
ai	as in "Thai"
air	as in "pair"
ao	as in "Mao Zedong"
ay	as in "day"
er	as in "enter"
ew	as in "few"
oh	as in "go"
oo	as in "boot"
OO	as in "book"
oy	as in "toy"
g	as in "give"
ng	as in "sing"

These sounds have no close equivalents in English:

eu	can be likened to a sound of disgust - the sound could be written as "errgh"
bp	a single sound between a "b" and a "p"
dt	a single sound between a "d" and a "t"

Note that when "p,""t," and "k" occur at the end of Thai words, the sound is "swallowed." Also note that many Thais use an "l" instead of an "r" sound

The Five Tones

Accents indicate the tone of each syllable.

no mark		The **mid tone** is voiced at the speaker's normal, even pitch.
á é í ó ú		The **high tone** is pitched slightly higher than the mid tone.
à è ì ò ù		The **low tone** is pitched slightly lower than the mid tone.
ǎ ě ǐ ǒ ǔ		The **rising tone** sounds like a questioning pitch, starting low and rising.
â ê î ô û		The falling tone sounds similar to an syllable word for emphasis.

In an Emergency

Help!	chôo-ay dôo-ay!
Fire!	fai mâi!
Where is the nearest hospital?	tâir-o-née mee rohng pa-yah-bahn yòo têe-nâi?
Call an ambulance!	rêe-uk rót pa-yah-bahn hâi nòy!
Call a doctor!	rêe-uk mŏr hâi nòy!
Call the police!	rêe-uk dtum ròo-ut hâi nòy!

Communication Essentials

Yes	châi or krúp/kà
No	mâi châi or mâi krúp/mâi kà
Please can you…?	chôo-ay
Thank you	kòrp-kOOn
No, thank you	mâi ao kòrp-kOOn
Excuse me/sorry	kŏr-tôht (krúp/kà)
Hello	sa-wùt dee (krúp/kà)
Goodbye	lah gòrn ná
What?	a-rai?
Why?	tum-mai?
Where?	têe nǎi?
How?	yung ngai?

Useful Phrases

How are you?	kOOn sa-bai dee reu (krúp/kà)?
Very well, thank you	sa-bai dee (krúp/kà)
How do I get to…?	…bpai yung-ngai?
Do you speak English?	kOOn pôot pah-săh ung-grìt bpen mǎi?
Could you speak slowly?	chôo-ay pôot cháh cháh nòy dâi mǎi?
I can't speak Thai.	pôot pah-săh tai mâi bpen

Useful Words

hot	rórn
cold	yen or nǎo
good	dee
bad	mâi dee
enough	por
open	bpèrt
closed	bpìt
left	sái
right	kwǎh
near	glâi
far	glai
straight ahead	yòo dtrong nâh
woman/women	pôo-yĭng
man/men	pôo-chai
child/children	dèk
entrance	tahng kâo
exit	tahng òrk
toilet	hôrng náhm

Keeping in Touch

Where is the nearest public telephone?	tâir-o née mee toh-ra-sùp yòo têe-nâi?
Can I call abroad from here?	ja toh bpai dtàhng bpra-tâyt jàhk têe nêe dâi mái?
Hello, this is… speaking.	hello (pŏm /dee-chún)…pôot (krúp/kà)
May I leave a message?	kŏr fàhk sùng a-rai nòy dâi mái?
I would like to speak to…	kŏr pôot gùp khun… nòy (krúp/kà)
local call	toh-ra-sùp pai nai tórng tìn
phone card	but toh-ra-sùp

Shopping

How much does this cost?	nêe rah-kah tâo-rài?
I would like…	dtôrng-gahn…
Do you have?	mee… mái?
I am just looking	chom doo tâo-nún
Do you take credit cards/travelers' checks?	rub but cray-dit/ chék dern tang mái?
What time do you open/close?	bpèrt/bpìt gèe mohng?
Can you ship this overseas?	sóng kõhng nee bpai dtàhng bpra-tâyt dài mái?
Could you lower the price a bit?	lót rah-kah nòy dâi mái?
How about…baht?	…bàht dâi mái?
That's a little expensive.	pairng bpai nòy
Will you go for… baht?	…bàht bpai mái?
I'll settle for… baht.	…bàht gôr láir-o-gun
cheap	tòok
expensive	pairng
Does it come in other colors?	mee sẽe èun èek mái?
black	sẽe dum
blue	sẽe núm ngern
green	sẽe kẽe-o
red	sẽe dairng
white	sẽe kão
yellow	sẽe lẽu-ung
gold	torng
silver	ngern
Thai silk	pâh-mãi tai
ladies' wear	sêu-pâh sa-dtree
bookstore	ráhn kãi núng-sẽu
department store	hâhng
pharmacy	ráhn kãi yah
market	dta-làht
newsstand	ráhn kãi núng-sẽu pim
shoe shop	ráhn kãi rorng táo
supermarket	sÓOp-bpèr-mah-gèt
tailor	ráhn dtùt sêu-a

Staying in a Hotel

Do you have a vacant room?	mee hôrng wâhng mái?
air-conditioned room	hôrng air
I have a reservation.	jorng hôrng wái láir-o
I'd like a room for one night/three nights.	(põm/dee-chún) ja púk yòo keun nèung/ sãhm keun
What is the charge per night?	kâh hôrng wun la tâo-rài?
I don't know yet how long I'll stay	mâi sâhp wâh ja yòo nahn tâo-rài
May I see the room first please?	kõr doo hôrng gòrn dâi mái?
May I leave some things in the safe?	kõr fàhk kõrng wái nai dtôo sáyf dâi mái?
Will you spray some mosquito repellent, please?	chôo-ay chèet yah gun yÓOng hâi nòy dâi mái?
double/twin room	hôrng kôo
single room	hôrng dèe-o
bedroom	hôrng norn
bill	bin
fan	pùt lom
hotel	rohng-rairm
key	gOOn-jair
manager	pôo-jùt-gahn
mosquito screen	mÓOng lôo-ut
shower	fúk boo-a
swimming pool	sà wâi náhm

Sightseeing

travel agent	bor-ri sùt num têe-o
tourist office	sũm-núk ngahn gahn tôrng têe-o
tourist police	dtum-ròo-ut tôrng têe-o
beach	háht or chai-háht
cliff	nâh pãh
festival	ngahn örk ráhn
hill/mountain	kão
historical park	ÒO-ta-yahn-bpra wùt sàht
island (koh)	gòr
lake	ta-lay sáhp
museum	pi-pít-ta-pun
national park	ÒO-ta yahn hãirng châht
palace	wang
park/garden	sõo-un
river	mâir náhm
ruins	boh-rahn sa-tãhn
temple (wat)	wút
Thai boxing	moo-ay tai
Thai massage	nôo-ut
trekking	gahn dern tahng táo
waterfall	náhm dtòk
zoo	sõo-un sàt

Transportation

When does the train for…leave?	rót fai bpai…òrt meu-rài?
How long does it take to get to…?	chái way-lah nahn tâo-rài bpai tẽung têe…?
A ticket to… please.	kõr dtõo-a bpai… nòy (krúp/kâ)
Which platform for the… train?	rót fai bpai… yòo chahn cha-lah nãi?
What station is this?	têe nêe sa-tãhn-nee a-rai?
I'd like to reserve a seat, please.	kõr jorng têe nûng
Where is the bus station?	sa-tãhn-nee rót may yòo têe-nãi?
Which buses go to…?	rót may sãi nãi bpai…?
What times does the bus for… leave?	rót may bpai… òrt gèe mohng?
Would you tell me when we get to… ?	tẽung… láir-o chôo-ay bòrk dóo-ay?
Is it far?	glai mái?
ticket	dtõo-a
air-conditioned bus	rót bprùp ah-gàht
airport	sa-nãhm bin
tour bus	rót too-a
train	rót fai
bus station	sa-tãhn-nee rót may
moped	rót mor-dter-sai
bicycle	rót jùk-gra-yahn
taxi	táirk-sêe

Eating Out

A table for two please.	kõr dtó sũm-rùp sõrng kon

May I see the menu?	*kŏr doo may-noo nòy?*
Do you have…?	*mee… mái?*
I'd like…	*kŏr…*
I didn't order this.	*nêe mâi dâi sùng (krúp/kà)*
Is it spicy?	*pèt mái?*
Not too spicy, ok?	*mâi ao pèt mâhk na*
I can eat Thai food.	*tahn ah-hăhn tai bpen*
May I have a glass of water, please.	*kŏr núm kăirng bplào gâir-o nèung*
Waiter/waitress!	*kOOn (krúp/kà)*
The check, please.	*kŏr bin nòy (krúp/kà)*
bottle	*kòo-ut*
chopsticks	*dta-gée-up*
drink(s)	*krêu-ung dèum*
fork	*sôrm*
glass	*gâir-o*
menu	*may-noo*
spoon	*chórn*

Menu Decoder

nòr mái	bamboo shoots
glóoy-ay	banana
néu-a woo-a	beef
bee-a	beer
dtôm	boiled
yâhng	char-grilled
gài	chicken
prík	chili
gah-fair	coffee
bpoo	crab
mèe gròrp	crispy noodles
gŏo-ay dtêe-o hâirng	dry noodles
bpèt	duck
tÓO-ree-un	durian
kài	egg
bplah	fish
king	ginger
núm kăirng bplào	iced water
ka-nÒOn	jackfruit
mâir-kŏhng	Mekong Whisky
hèt	mushroom
gŏo-ay dtêe-o-náhm	noodle soup
ma-la-gor	papaya
sùp-bpa-rót	pineapple
néu-a-mŏo	pork
kâo	rice
gŏo-ay dtêe-o	rice noodles
gÔOng	shrimp
núm see éw	soup
ah-hăhn wăhng	soy sauce
pùk ka-náh	spring greens
kâo-nĕe-o	sticky rice
kâo pôht	sweet corn
núm chah	tea
pùk	vegetables
náhm	water

Health

I do not feel well	*róa-sèuk mâi sa-bai*
It hurts here.	*jèp dtrong née*
I have a fever.	*dtoo-a-rórn bpen kâi*
sore throat	*jèp kor*
stomach ache	*bpòo-ut tórng*
vomit	*ah-jee-un*
asthma	*rôhk hèut*
cough	*ai*
diabetes	*rôhk bao wăhn*

diarrhea	*tórng sĕe-a*
dizzy	*wee-un hŏo-a*
dysentry	*rôhk bìt*
fever	*kâi*
headache	*bpòo-ut hŏo-a*
aspirin	*air-sa-bprin or yah-gàir kâi*
doctor	*mŏr*
dentist	*tun-dta-pâirt or mŏr fun*
hospital	*rohng pa-yah-bahn*
injection	*chèet yah*
medicine	*yah*
prescription	*bai sùng yah*
How many tablets do I take?	*dtôrng gin yah gèe mét dtòr krúng*
I'm allergic to…	*(pŏm/dee-chún) páir…*

Numbers

0	*sŏon*
1	*nèung*
2	*sŏrng*
3	*săhm*
4	*sèe*
5	*hâh*
6	*hòk*
7	*jèt*
8	*bpàirt*
9	*gâo*
10	*sìp*
11	*sìp-èt*
12	*sìp-sŏrng*
13	*sìp-săhm*
14	*sìp-sèe*
15	*sìp-hâh*
16	*sìp-hòk*
17	*sìp-jét*
18	*sìp-bpàirt*
19	*sìp-gâo*
20	*yêe-sìp*
30	*săhm-sìp*
40	*sèe-sìp*
50	*hâh-sìp*
60	*hòk-sìp*
70	*jèt-sìp*
80	*bpàirt-sìp*
90	*gâo-sìp*
100	*nèung róy*
1,000	*nèung pun*
10,000	*nèung mèun*
100,000	*nèung săirn*

Time

one minute	*nèung nah-tee*
one hour	*nèung chôo-a mohng*
half an hour	*krêung chôo-a mohng*
Sunday	*wun ah-tít*
Monday	*wun jun*
Tuesday	*wun ung-kahn*
Wednesday	*wun pÓOt*
Thursday	*wun pa-réu-hùt*
Friday	*wun sÒOk*
Saturday	*wun săo*
a day	*neung wun*
a week	*nèung ah-tít*
a weekend	*sÒOt sùp-pah-dah*
a month	*nèung deu-un*
a year	*nèung bpee*